Tales from the Taiwanese

World Folklore Advisory Board

Tales from the Taiwanese

Retold By
Gary Marvin Davison

World Folklore Series

LIBRARIES
U N L I M I T E D
A Member of the Greenwood Publishing Group

Westport, Connecticut • London

Library of Congress Cataloging-in-Publication Data

Davison, Gary Marvin, 1951–
    Tales form the Taiwanese / Retold by Gary Marvin Davison.
      p. cm. — (World folklore series)
    Includes bibliographical references and index.
    ISBN 1–59158–111–7
    1. Tales—Taiwan. I. Title. II. Series.
  GR338.D38 2004
  398.2'095124'9—dc22   2004044197

British Library Cataloguing in Publication Data is available.

Library of Congress Catalog Card Number: 2004044197
ISBN: 1-59158-111-7

First published in 2004

Libraries Unlimited, 88 Post Road West, Westport, CT 06881
A Member of the Greenwood Publishing Group, Inc.
www.lu.com

Printed in the United States of America

The paper used in this book complies with the Permanent Paper Standard issued by the National Information Standards Organization (Z39.48–1984).

10 9 8 7 6 5 4 3 2 1

Contents

Introduction

Taiwan is an island with a unique culture and a highly successful economy. It is one of those places in the world that for centuries came under the control of foreigners, even as its people were developing an identity separate from any of those outside governing groups. The world is full of societies that did not emerge as independent nations until the nineteenth or twentieth centuries. These countries include South American nations, such as Brazil, Venezuela, and Argentina; European nations, such as Latvia, Slovakia, and Croatia; Central Asian nations, such as Uzbekistan, Azerbaijan, and Kyrgystan; Middle Eastern (West Asian) nations, such as Jordan, Israel, and Iraq; and Southeast Asian nations, such as Indonesia, Singapore, and the Philippines. Even the United States did not declare independence from Great Britain until 1776, and it only had its status as a nation recognized with the Treaty of Paris of 1783, following the American Revolution.

For centuries, Taiwan was occupied exclusively by its original settlers, people who today are known as "aborigines." Then, from the seventeenth century forward, Dutch, Spanish, Manchu, Japanese, and Chinese people competed for control of the island. The ancestors of most people on Taiwan today came originally from China, during that same span of time, beginning in the seventeenth century, when Taiwan was governed by the various outsider groups. Taiwan was then controlled by Japan from 1895 to 1945, and from 1945 until 2000 was governed by a political party, the Guomindang, that had escaped to Taiwan after losing a civil war to the Chinese Communist Party, which since 1949 has controlled China. Throughout the twentieth century, then, Taiwan's history unfolded separately from that of China, and its people came to look upon themselves first as Taiwanese, people whose deeper roots were mostly in China but who, over the course of decades and even centuries, had developed an identity only partially connected to the land of their ancestral origins.

Today there is an ongoing effort on the island to state in clear terms what makes Taiwan's identity unique and what part aborigine, European, Chinese, Japanese, and American influences have played in shaping the island's distinct culture. Up until the 1990s, the Guomindang discouraged the production of books, plays, and art that focused on a uniquely Taiwanese identity, but in the last ten years, numerous books, works of art, and public discussions have focused on just that topic. After the victory of Democratic Progressive Party member Chen Shuibian in the presidential election of 2000, the number of cultural productions and public forums focused on Taiwanese culture have increased greatly.

I have lived in Taiwan for two extended periods (1980–1981 and 1988–1990), and I have visited many other times, including multiweek trips in the summers of 1995, 1998, and 2003. I have witnessed the political transformation that has allowed discussion of Taiwan's independent identity and its unique cultural life to flourish. This book focuses on Taiwan as Taiwan—an island whose culture owes much to Chinese civilization but which has been shaped by many forces and has a history that has unfolded differently from that of China. There are a few short story collections and novels from Taiwan that have been rendered in English, but there are none that focus on traditional folktales and stories specifically from the Taiwanese, as opposed to the Chinese, tradition. You are reading, then, a groundbreaking work, a book that presents the folktale tradition of Taiwan to an English-reading audience. The tales are retold with children of kindergarten through upper-elementary age in mind. Children in the fourth, fifth, and sixth grades should be able to read these stories on their own or, for the earlier age groups, to respond with delight to a teacher's or parent's reading of them. Particularly because these tales are reaching an English-reading audience for the first time, but also because the stories are engaging to people of any age, adults will also find this book an appealing read, as well as a source for classroom and bedtime reading sessions with their students and children.

The stories in this book were collected from a variety of tellers during my second period of residence (1988–1990) on Taiwan. During that time, I was conducting research on the lives and economy of Taiwanese farmers. For one three-month period, I found myself sitting in a hair salon patronized by both women and men in the small village of Shezi in Tainan County, getting to know villagers and listening to their tales of events both real and imagined. One day, the young woman who ran the hair salon brought with her a book that she had read in middle school. The book was, of course, in Chinese, bearing a title that translates into English as *Popular Tales from Taiwan* (the romanization of the Chinese title is *Taiwan minjian gushi*). It had been produced by an anonymous author and publisher at a time when the Guomindang discouraged, and sometimes punished, those who produced such works focused on the particular culture of Taiwan. The young woman's teacher had introduced the book and its tales to her students at some personal risk, but she had managed to do so without drawing a response from local authorities. As I sat in the hair salon, I reviewed these stories with villagers. I found that adults and many children knew most of these tales apart from their existence in the book, for they are those that have been told by many people over the course of Taiwanese history. Most of them are an engrained part of Taiwanese culture, just as tales such as "Little Red Riding Hood," "Cinderella," and "The Three Little Pigs" are familiar to virtually everybody in Western societies.

Like the tales from the Western tradition, these stories have numerous variations, according to the preferred versions and the embellishments of different tellers. In presenting the tales, I have endeavored to blend the most engaging features from the various tellings in such a way as to delight and inform a Western audience with the liveliness, color, humor, values, and cultural perspectives that animate the Taiwanese cultural tradition. The book is organized to focus on certain aspects of the stories and the culture that they reflect. Thus, the stories fall into one of six parts: "Taiwanese Values," "Taiwanese Religion and Ethics," "Taiwanese Tales of Natural Origins," "Taiwanese Sayings and Their Origins," "Legends and Historical Tales," and "Taiwanese Humor."

Before introducing the tales, the book offers a summary of Taiwan's history that lends more detail to the observations made in the opening paragraphs of this introduction. Certain figures, such as Koxinga, and certain subethnic groups, such as the Quanzhou and Zhangzhou people, that are important to know about before reading the tales are covered in the historical summary. At the end of each tale, teachers, parents, students, and other readers will find questions for discussion and activities flowing from certain topics and themes in the story that will be of interest to children and adults alike. Similarly, a feature near the end of the book offers recipes from Taiwan that all lovers of good food will appreciate.

The tales in this book are told lovingly and with great respect for a people whom I have come to admire over twenty years of association with them. My goal is to engage readers in such a way that they will both delight in, and learn about, the way the Taiwanese people think about social values, religion, nature, history, and the use of language in tales both to establish certain life principles and to just plain have fun. If this goal is accomplished, as I trust it will be, then you the reader will have come to learn a great deal about, and to appreciate, the culture and history of a people who today form one of the most dynamic and exciting societies in the world.

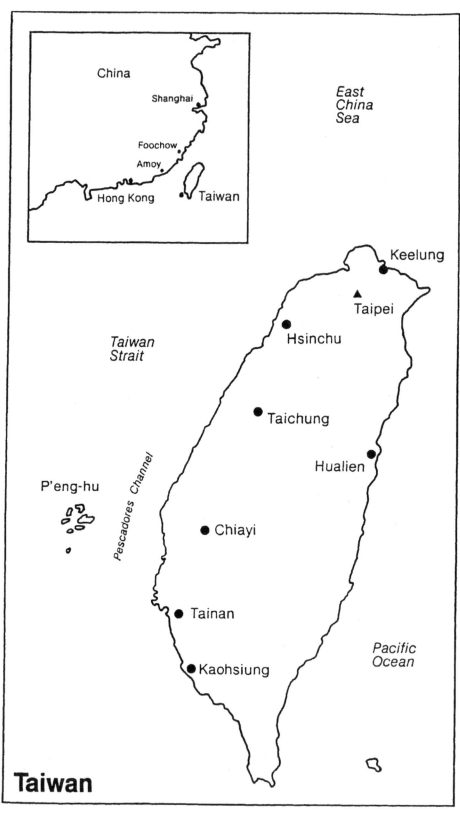

Map of Taiwan (Government Information Office, Taipei, ROC).

Taiwan's History

People are at the heart of history, so it is important to understand whom we mean when we refer to the "Taiwanese" as we learn about Taiwan's history and culture. In the course of many centuries, several different groups of people have settled on Taiwan and today contribute to the Taiwanese population. The first people who came to Taiwan are those known today as the "aborigines." These people came to Taiwan about four thousand years ago. Some people who study the prehistory of Taiwan and other islands in the southern Pacific Ocean think that people who came to live in Indonesia, the Philippines, and many other islands of the Pacific came first to Taiwan before moving on to other places. Each aboriginal group on Taiwan speaks a different language. An aborigine who knows only her or his own language cannot understand what a person from another aboriginal group is saying. But these aborigine languages do belong to the same general family of languages, known as the Malayo-Polynesian language group, which includes languages spoken by the people of Malaysia, Indonesia, and many islands of the Pacific Ocean. Most aborigine children go to schools in which Mandarin Chinese is the language used by teachers. This enables them to communicate in a language that most young aborigines and most Chinese people on Taiwan now understand.

Until the seventeenth century, the aborigines were the dominant population on Taiwan. There are at least nine aboriginal tribes who remain on the island today. Virtually all scholars agree that the nine aboriginal groups different enough from one another to be considered unique and distinct communities include the Ami, Paiwan, Taya, Bunun, Puyuma, Tsou, Yami, and Saisiat people. Some scholars say that two other groups, the Taroko and the Thao, are distinctive enough to expand the total number of discreet aboriginal groups active on Taiwan today to eleven. Traditionally, the aborigines of Taiwan were mainly hunter-gatherers and fishers. They also farmed on a small scale, producing such crops as rice, sugarcane, yams, and taro. They did not use plow animals, but they did raise dogs, pigs, and chickens. The aborigines lived in self-governing and self-sufficient villages in which people were generally treated as equals, with little difference as to social-class status. Their houses generally had thatched roofs over structures made of

1

various natural materials, especially bamboo and wood from Taiwan's abundant forests. Men did most of the hunting, while women planted crops and gathered plants that could be eaten for food. Rigid boundaries were not established to close off one aborigine group from another, in the manner of modern nations, but certain areas were known to be occupied primarily by a particular aboriginal group for residence, hunting, fishing, and the gathering and cultivation of food. Young warriors were proud of their ability to defend these zones of usage from unwanted intrusion by other groups.

There are about 300,000 aborigines on Taiwan today. They live throughout the island but are especially concentrated in tribal areas set aside for them by the government of Taiwan, much as the government of the United States set aside reservations for Native Americans. And, as was the case with Native Americans in the United States, many aborigines resented efforts on the part of the government to constrain their lives within rigid boundaries and force them to become more like people of the dominant culture. There have been ongoing tensions between the aborigines and the great majority of people, who are of Chinese ancestry. But on the Taiwan of the early twenty-first century, where even many people of Chinese ancestry think of themselves first as Taiwanese, rather than Chinese, these first peoples of the island are increasingly respected for their long residence on Taiwan and their contributions to its culture.

Today most of Taiwan's population is made up of people known as the "Han Chinese," which refers to that majority of people whose style of government, art, and social organization have dominated life on mainland China since the time of the Han dynasty. Although mainland China has its own aboriginal and minority peoples, Han Chinese make up about 95 percent of the population, and they are those whom people usually mean when they refer simply to the "Chinese."

Within Taiwan, the Han Chinese population is divided into three main groups: the Hakka, the Fujianese, and the "mainlanders." The Hakka are people who first lived in northern China but eventually settled in Guangdong province in southern coastal China. Like the Fujianese, they first came to Taiwan in significant numbers in the seventeenth century. The Fujianese are those who came from another southern coastal province of China, the province of Fujian. The Fujianese are themselves divided into two subgroups whose local loyalties and slightly different customs sometimes led each to look at the other as a group apart, and even as a competitor. The two Fujianese subgroups are the Quanzhou and Zhangzhou people, named for the districts in Fujian province from which they came.

The Han Chinese known as the "mainlanders" came to Taiwan long after either of the two Fujianese subgroups. Mainlanders are those who came to Taiwan from the late 1940s on, fleeing China for various reasons connected to the outcome of the 1946–1949 Chinese Civil War. The mainlanders came from various provinces of China, and some mainlanders identify strongly with the villages, counties, and provinces from which they came. They shared in common, though, certain experiences during the Chinese Civil War and the fact of their relatively recent arrival on Taiwan. Until at least the 1980s, mainlanders were favored with the best positions in public affairs and government-sponsored businesses and industries. Because of this, there have been significant tensions between the mainlanders and those Han Chinese who had been living on Taiwan long before the 1940s (aborigines, Hakka, and both subgroups of the Fujianese). For several decades beginning in the 1940s, when people spoke of the "Taiwanese" they really meant the Hakka people and the Quanzhou and Zhangzhou Fujianese, leaving out both the aborigines and the mainlanders. On Taiwan of the early twenty-first century, however, the trend is to refer to all of these people who live on the island as Taiwanese. Although there remain cultural differences among them, all of these people have now lived on Taiwan long enough, and share enough in common, to regard themselves as distinct from those Han Chinese and others now living on the Chinese mainland.

Han Chinese people first began coming to Taiwan in greater numbers toward the end of the Ming dynasty (1368–1644). During the last several decades of that period, Manchus from the area now known as mainland China's "Northeast" launched an effort to take control of all of China. By 1644, the Manchus established the last of China's imperial dynasties, the Qing (pronounced something like "chying"). But the contest for control of southern China lasted another forty years. This brought the devastation of war to a southern Chinese people already struggling with the effects of periodic floods, drought, and famine. Because of these various circumstances, many people from southern China sought homes away from the mainland. Taiwan was one of those places. Most of these immigrants took up occupations common to their ancestors in Guangdong and Fujian, usually farming but also fishing, and eventually people established towns where shopkeepers, artisans, and traders practiced their professions.

When Chinese first started coming to Taiwan in significant numbers, they found that Dutch people representing the government of the Netherlands controlled the island. During the middle years of the seventeenth century, the Netherlands fought another European country, Spain, for control of Taiwan. The Dutch occupied southern Taiwan in 1624, then in 1642 they drove the Spaniards from their forts in northern Taiwan. During the next twenty years, the Dutch colonial government encouraged Chinese settlement of the island, providing seeds, tools, and oxen to help Chinese farmers produce rice and sugar. The Dutch then heavily taxed the crops produced by the farmers and gained great profit from selling rice and, especially, sugar to other people in Southeast and East Asia, particularly the Japanese.

Meanwhile, in southern China, various people who remained loyal to the Ming dynasty continued the struggle against the Manchus. One of these loyalists was a man by the name of Zheng Chenggong, also known as Guo Xingye, a title given to him by a Ming dynasty emperor. Europeans pronounced this title "Koxinga," the name often given in English language accounts of this hero.

Why was Koxinga a hero? Why do many Taiwanese still regard him as such today? This is because during 1661–1662 Koxinga mounted an attack on the Dutch and drove them from the island of Taiwan. Because most people who came to be known as the "Taiwanese" came originally from mainland China, the victory of fellow Chinese over a European colonial power is remembered as a great triumph. Many entertaining legends came to be told about the great power of Koxinga. You will read about some of these in story number nineteen, "Iron Anvil Mountain and the Well of Koxinga."

Koxinga died soon after he took control of Taiwan, but his family ruled the island until 1683. In that year the Manchus, now in secure control of southern China, launched an attack on the Zheng family's military forces. The Manchus won the struggle and established a government on Taiwan that would last until 1895. During the years from 1683 until 1895, thousands of Hakka people from Guangdong, and Quanzhou and Zhangzhou people from Fujian, made the difficult hundred-mile journey across the Taiwan Strait from mainland China. You will read a story about one of the people whose ancestors came from Quanzhou in story number four, "Justice Comes to Elder Sister Lintou."

Taiwanese society and economy became ever more sophisticated in the years of Qing dynasty rule. The Taiwanese proved to be exceptionally hardworking people. They produced great quantities of rice and sugar for sale to traders from mainland China. The aborigines were excellent hunters who kept Taiwanese traders in large supplies of venison (deer meat) and deer hides for sale to people from mainland China. Merchants set up shop in towns such as Lugang, on the western Taiwan coast, to sell goods imported from mainland China and produced by craftspeople on Taiwan itself.

In 1895, the Japanese gained control over Taiwan. Taiwan was one of the places that the Qing dynasty had to give up when it lost a war to the Japanese during 1894–1895. By this time, Japan had become a very modern place, with factory production and military might to equal that of European powers such as Great Britain and Germany. The Japanese were tough rulers who taxed the Taiwanese heavily and dictated what agricultural and industrial goods would be produced. But the Japanese also brought more modern conveniences such as roads, railroads, telephones, telegraphs, and electrical power to the island.

Back on the mainland, the World War II years of 1939–1945 were terrible for the Chinese people. Japan also took control of much of mainland China in 1937, then up until 1945 struggled against those Chinese determined to drive the Japanese conquerors from their land. When the Japanese conceded defeat in World War II in 1945, they were forced to leave both China and Taiwan. For a while, the government of a man named Chiang Kai-shek ruled both China and Taiwan. Then, in 1949, Chiang and his Guomindang (Kuomintang) government and army lost the civil war that they had been forced to fight against the soldiers of the Chinese Communist Party, led by Mao Zedong. At that point, Chiang and his supporters fled to Taiwan. Chiang Kai-shek served as president of the Republic of China on Taiwan until he died in 1975. Then his son, Chiang Ching-kuo, served as president until his own death in 1988. Another Guomindang president, Lee Teng-hui, held the office until the year 2000.

During those years from 1949 until 2000, the Taiwanese people worked hard to make Taiwan one of the most economically advanced places in the world. Guomindang policies built upon the strong economic foundation laid by the Japanese and helped to make the island very productive in both agriculture and industry. But the Guomindang was a tough ruling force that did not allow democracy to exist on Taiwan. Chiang Ching-kuo encouraged a bit more popular participation and freedom than did his father, and Lee Teng-hui attempted to shape a much more complete democratic society than either of the Chiangs. The National Assembly of Taiwan, controlled by the Guomindang, chose Lee Teng-hui as president after Chiang Ching-kuo died in 1988. In 1996, Lee won the first popular election for president, an exercise in democracy that he himself had helped to bring about. By the time of the presidential election of 2000, however, the Taiwanese people were ready for new leadership. Lee Teng-hui was personally popular, but his party was not. Lee retired, and the Guomindang candidate who ran in his place lost to Chen Shuibian, leader of the Democratic Progressive Party. Today Taiwan is a full democracy with highly competitive elections for the legislature, as well as the presidency.

Taiwanese culture has been shaped by the aborigines and by the Hakka, Quanzhou, and Zhangzhou people of mainland China. The aborigines give other Taiwanese the sense that their island has a long prehistory and history that had no important link to the Chinese mainland until the seventeenth century. The crafts and clothes of the aborigines tend to be of very colorful and exquisite artisanship. The distinctive canoes of the Yami people, with their finely painted red, white, and black design; the skilled musicianship and wind instruments produced by the Bunun people; and the fine woodwork in housing design and articles of symbolic and practical use evident in the culture of the Paiwan are among the many examples of aborigine craft expertise that contribute greatly to the rich artistic and cultural mix on Taiwan. Similarly, the Hakka farmers wear distinctive cloth hats very different from the conical straw hats of Fujianese farmers. Hakka women never bound their feet, as was the custom in many Fujianese homes; this may be taken as a symbol of a famous independent streak for which the Hakka are known. Their spoken language is also different from the Minnan language of the Fujianese. While the Guomindang was still in control, Mandarin was used exclusively on television broadcasts, but today Mandarin shares the airwaves with Hakka and Minnan. The Quanzhou and Zhangzhou people of Fujian share a common language, and it is they who have built most of the temples and houses that one sees in all regions of Taiwan. They share a highly similar culture and heritage, and they have in common religious and philosophical beliefs rooted in the traditions of Buddhism, Daoism (Taoism), and Confucianism. Historically, though, their difference in geographic origins frequently led people from Quanzhou and Zhangzhou to form separate religious, cultural, and business associations. Today these distinctions between the two main Fujianese groups are not as important as they once were, but evidence that a certain person has roots to a particular village in Quanzhou or Zhangzhou is still a matter of interest and ancestral pride.

Taiwanese culture has also been shaped by fifty years of Japanese rule. There is a great deal of physical evidence of the historical presence of the Japanese on Taiwan. The presidential building and many other government offices in Taibei and elsewhere across the island provide sturdily built reminders of a tough but highly competent Japanese colonial rule. People who are today in their seventies and older were educated primarily in schools using Japanese as the medium of instruction, and many of these older people are at least as comfortable with Japanese dress, household customs, and language as they are with Chinese culture. The nation of Japan continues to be a leader in matters of culture and, especially, business and industry, which many people on Taiwan see as a model for themselves and other East Asians.

Those mainlanders who accompanied the Guomindang to the island from the late 1940s came from all over China and introduced their own styles of cooking, talking, and acting into Taiwanese society, and they, too, contribute to the cultural mix that today defines the "Taiwanese." The cuisines of Beijing, Shanghai, Canton, and Chengdu—cities of northern, eastern, southern, and western China, respectively—add to the delight of eating on this island famous for its wonderful food. Similarly, the mainlanders brought with them the unique opera of Beijing and a tradition in music, dance, painting, sculpture, and calligraphy representing one of the great civilizations in world history. Taibei's National Palace Museum provides powerful examples of this cultural tradition, housing the world's finest collection of Chinese art.

American influence has also been great, because for many years the United States government aided and advised the Guomindang. United States economic aid greatly assisted the government and people of Taiwan in attaining their astounding economic success of the past four decades. American movies, clothes, television shows, and fast-food restaurants greatly influence contemporary Taiwanese popular culture. Many Taiwanese young people go the United States to attend colleges and universities, bringing back American- and European-influenced perspectives on doing business, conducting scholarly investigations, building roads and buildings, and establishing strong democratic institutions.

With such varied cultural influences evident in the history and in the present society of Taiwan, many people on Taiwan today consider Chinese culture to be just one of the many elements that have historically defined and now define what it means to be Taiwanese. The government on Taiwan is still officially called the "Republic of China," while the government on mainland China is known as the "People's Republic of China." The mainland government claims that Taiwan should be one of its territories. Most people on Taiwan do not want the island to come under mainland Chinese control. Many see Taiwan as a nation in its own right and would prefer that the island be known as the "Republic of Taiwan." But officially declaring Taiwanese independence would greatly anger the leaders of the People's Republic of China. So even though leaders such as Lee Teng-hui and Chen Shuibian do see Taiwan as an independent nation, they and most others have not declared Taiwanese independence. They do not want the war with mainland China that such a declaration might bring.

Taiwan today has a population of about 23 million people. On an island that is just about 245 miles long and 90 miles wide, with a thick mountainous spine running from north to south where few people live, this gives Taiwan one of the world's highest population densities. But it is an exceptionally well-educated, hardworking population and, although there is a tendency for people to move to big cities, the population remains well distributed in five large cities (Taibei, Jilong, Taizhong, Tainan, and Gaoxiong) and many towns stretching across Taiwan. From industries spread across the island, Taiwan's industrious workforce continues to produce textiles, clothing, and processed foods, and it has over the last two decades become one of the world's leaders in the production of high-technology goods from the electronics and computer industries. Political democratization has brought with it relaxation of controls on outside media influences, so that virtually all Taiwanese, particularly the young, are affected greatly by the images and messages delivered through movies, television, radio, books, and magazines that originate in the United States, Japan, and cosmopolitan centers across the world. Taiwan will almost certainly continue to be one of the most economically productive and successful places in the world. With its own high level of communications technology and its openness to the outside world, the island will continue to be a major economic force, and very much a part of the worldwide exchange of goods and ideas. For the time, though, its future governmental status remains very much an unresolved question.

Just as our folktales reflect our values and beliefs, so, too, do the tales of other cultures offer insight into their ways of thinking. By reading the stories in this book, you will have fun while gaining knowledge of the way the Taiwanese people think about religion, work, social customs, family relationships, and what is truly important in life. You will learn more about these people who have shaped the history of a unique island.

Part One

Taiwanese Values

One

Have you ever known anyone who just could not be content with being very smart, or tall, or strong, but also constantly had to try to prove that she or he was in some way better than a classmate, or even a good friend? The Taiwanese have a tale about the problems that this attitude can bring, based on what happened to a once-mighty mountain.

Little-Bitty Banping Mountain

At the northwest corner of Gaoxiong, Taiwan's second largest city, there lies a little-bitty sawed-off looking mountain by the name of Banping. The name *Banping* means "half a peak" in Mandarin Chinese. Banping is still pretty enough, its slopes covered with tropical trees and plants shining in multicolored glory under the brilliant tropical sun of southern Taiwan. But once Banping Mountain was a lofty and majestic peak, towering over the county that includes Gaoxiong. Now, on an island where the tallest mountains reach to 4,000 meters, Banping stretches only to 200 meters at its highest point. How did this once-mighty mountain come to be so small? Geologists of the island have their own answer, while storytellers have another. The version told by storytellers goes like this:

One eventful day long ago when Banping Mountain was tall and impressive, it offered a challenge to Jade Mountain, another high peak in the region: "You think that you are so high and mighty, but you're nothing compared to me. We must have a contest to prove who is taller!"

Now Jade Mountain was a proud peak, but very confident in its own strength and imposing stature. It really felt no need to prove its grandeur, for its impressive appearance was clear to anyone who gazed at its towering slopes. So Jade Mountain said to its would-be opponent, "Banping, my friend, what need do either of us have to show off our might? We are both naturally impressive enough. Let us be content to stand close together as brothers, offering our tall beauty to all who will gaze upon us. What does it matter if I am a bit taller than you, or if you are a bit taller than I? What embarrassment should either of us feel if we prove to be the shorter? And, in any case, how would two mountains so close in size truly determine which is taller?"

But Banping fancied itself the world's tallest mountain. It was shamelessly boastful about its height. It arrogantly replied to Jade Mountain, "I am so tall that if someone were to place three pieces of tofu [bean curd] at my highest point, those pieces would touch the sky. Can you show that you are so tall that you could touch the sky in this way?"

In and beyond the skies to which this mountain braggart referred, the Heavenly Emperor was listening to Banping's boast. The Heavenly Emperor grew more angry with each word spoken by this showoff of a mountain. For who presided over nature and all of creation, who determined the conditions by which things thrived or declined? Who could boast that she or he held any might at all apart from what the Heavenly Emperor decided should be and continue to be?

Thus, as Banping finished its boastful challenge to the securely confident but humble Jade Mountain, the Heavenly Emperor commanded the God of Thunder to act in the fullness of its power. An enormous blast shook the skies and came straight toward the spot in Gaoxiong County where Banping stood so tall and overly proud. In a flash, the sound of Banping Mountain breaking in two rattled Heaven and Earth. One half of Banping slid into the depths of the ocean, while the other half rose, then collapsed back onto solid ground.

Never again would Banping be in a position to boast or to issue the kind of challenge that it had arrogantly sent toward Jade Mountain. Banping appears to the modern viewer a mere fragment of its former self. So haughty in its days of grandeur, Banping now seems little more than an oversized hill.

Questions for Discussion

1. Banping actually had a great deal for which to be thankful. It was a tall mountain in a beautiful part of an island generally know for its stunning natural scenery. Banping could look out from its great height on forest, field, and sea. It had a good friend with which to talk and share all that they both had in abundance. Sometimes we should just take a moment to appreciate all of the good things that we have. For what are you particularly thankful for in life?

2. Is it possible that Banping is actually happier as a small mountain than it was when it was so tall, but also so arrogant? Explain your answer.

Suggestions for Class Activities

1. Have the students conduct an investigation focused on the world's tallest peaks. Divide the class into six groups, with each group taking one of six continents: North America, South America, Europe, Asia, Africa, or Australia. Have each group investigate and report on the age, circumstances of formation, and characteristics of the mountains and mountain systems in each of these continents. Through sculpture, painting, or some other artistic medium, have each group illustrate the five tallest peaks on each of the continents. As a class, calculate the percentage difference between peaks. Are there any correlations between height and age or formation? Between other characteristics? Discuss.

2. Have students investigate the climate of Taiwan and the ecosystems of some of the mountain areas on the island, including Banping Mountain, if possible. What types of plant and animal life reside in the Taiwan mountains? Do different animals live in different mountains? Assign various plants and animals from the research to each student, and have them write a report about it, with an illustration, to share with the class.

3. Have students locate Banping Mountain on the map and then create a geographic map of Taiwan.

Two

How many people do you know who have names given to them for a special reason? Here is a story that tells how one such person got his name.

The Much-Deserved Good Fortune of Li Menhuan

There was once a very rich local magistrate by the name of Zhang Fushan who had three daughters. The eldest two daughters had already been married to young men from families of means, leaving only the youngest, Yu Zhi, unmarried. All three daughters had grown up to be extraordinarily lovely and highly intelligent young women and thus had many suitors. But Yu Zhi had rejected the attentions of each young man who had come calling. In trying to make some sense of the situation, the official asked his youngest daughter why she had sent each suitor away with a negative answer. She replied in this manner:

"Your daughter understands papa's desire to see her find a good husband. She knows that sooner or later she must marry and move away from her village of birth. Otherwise, she would be a burden to father and could never provide him the brideprice that he deserves to help repay the cost of raising her. [Note: The brideprice is the amount of money or gift of equivalent value that the groom's family gives the bride's family.] Your daughter understands that papa knows many rich and powerful families who could provide a husband who would bring much honor to her family. Yet father's daughter would rather marry a hardworking and frugal man, not a young man who merely collects rents for his wealthy family. She has no desire to marry a lazy and idle gentleman whose only attractive features are his money and his family name.

"Often such a fellow squanders his family's money and in time his fame turns to shame. Such a fate is often ordained by Heaven, just as a poor person's fate may turn out to bring a better life than one might expect. Every person's fate is ordained by Heaven. A poor person's luck may one day take a turn for the better. He may all of a sudden become a man of wealth and renown. Your daughter feels deep in her heart that her own fate lies with a diligent man of humble circumstances. She feels that in the long run such a man will reward her patience, and that of father, with an even better life than their family has previously known."

The official could not bring himself to understand this point of view. He considered his daughter to be defying him in a most unfilial way [neglectful of one's duties, or demonstrating disrespectful behavior, toward a parent]. The more he thought of his daughter's attitude toward marriage, the angrier he became. And this anger showed when he said to her, "So, then, according to these words of yours, it would be your wish that I seek a poor man for your husband? This is the future that you desire for yourself?"

Before Yu Zhi could reply, a peddler by the name of Li Buzhi came calling. Mr. Li lived in a broken-down hut on the edge of the city. His main occupation was catching frogs, which he sold in the local market town and by going door-to-door. Seeing that this man arrived in tattered clothing to sell his frogs, Zhang Fushan quickly seized upon an idea. He invited Li Buzhi inside and said to him, "Mr. Li, have you married yet?"

Li Buzhi replied, "Honorable one, please don't make fun of a poor one such as myself by asking this sort of question. I am so poor that I don't get enough to eat myself. How would I ever attract a young woman to be my wife, when I myself have to struggle just to get by?"

Zhang Fushan replied, "Well, that's fine, then. I'll just give you my youngest daughter, Yu Zhi here, to be your wife."

Li Buzhi was so astonished that his reaction was to turn and run back in the direction from which he had come. Never in his wildest dreams had he thought that the magistrate would play this awful trick on him. Yet three days later, here came the young woman Yu Zhi with the bag of white rice that her mother had prepared for her as a gift to her prospective in-laws. To the jeers of her kinsmen, she went trodding off to the poor hut of the frog-catcher Li Buzhi. A simple ceremony was held. The humble frog-catcher gained the young wife that he had been so sure he could not have. Yu Zhi, though, did not resent any of this at all. The very next day she put in a hard day's work, diligently beginning her new life as a poor young wife.

One day very soon after his marriage to Yu Zhi, Li Buzhi went off to work as usual in high hopes of catching a big bunch of frogs. But his luck was not as great as he had hoped. He didn't catch a single frog. He was so dispirited that he turned to go back home. But just as he did so, a white rabbit darted before him. "Maybe this is my day to catch a fat rabbit instead of a scrawny frog!" he exclaimed.

He gave chase, but the rabbit was too swift for Li, who reached with out-stretched hands that came up empty. The rabbit escaped through a hole, into which Li Buzhi thrust himself in the hopes of catching the fleeing animal. But once inside the hole, all he saw were black bricks lying all around. He grabbed one of these bricks, scrambled out of the hole, and went back home.

When Yu Zhi got a look at the black brick that her husband had in tow, she let out with a yelp of delight. She knew that this was a rare brick of black gold. When she told him this, Li Buzhi leapt into the air in utter joy. Then he ran as fast as he could back to the cave where he had discovered the treasure. But when he crawled back down through the hole, no bricks of black gold came into sight as he scanned the cave. He rubbed his eyes, looked all around the cave again, and this time brought into focus another interesting but very different sight. It was a dignified old gentleman, who soon exclaimed loudly, "Hey, this treasure belongs to Li Menhuan. Your good fortune extends only to the single brick. I must ask you to leave!"

Li Buzhi thought these comments from the old man very strange. He knew no one named Menhuan, certainly not in his family. But soon his thoughts turned to his good fortune. He had not been able to find the great wealth that he had imagined when he thought that he could take away a great number of those valu-able bricks. But one such brick was enough to improve greatly the life of one so poor. From the time that Li Buzhi found the black gold brick, his life underwent quite a favorable transformation.

It wasn't long before Yu Zhi gave birth to a boy. According to Taiwanese custom, when the child reached the age of one month, the young mother bought her baby boy a number of presents and asked her husband to take their son to her family to announce the wonderful news of his birth. When Master Zhang saw how lively and adorable this young boy was, he took him in his arms and gave him a big hug. But the child immediately began to weep uncontrollably. The mag-istrate attempted to distract his grandson by strolling toward the door and giving several raps on the ringed door knocker. When the child heard the sound made by the knocker, he quit crying and began to laugh in delight. The official asked Li Buzhi, "Does this child have a name yet?"

"Not yet," replied Li Buzhi.

"Well, then, I'll choose one for him! The child laughed with such delight when he saw and heard the door knocker, I say that we name him Menhuan" [the Chinese name for a ringed door knocker of the sort that had delighted the child].

This of course made Li Buzhi think of what the old gentleman had told him in the cave. He took the child from his father-in-law and hurried back home and reported all that had happened to his wife. He then raced to the cave with the child in his arms. And as he suspected might happen, the rare black gold bricks once more appeared. From that day forward, Li Buzhi was a wealthy man.

In the aftermath of this transformation into a man of wealth and prestige, Li Buzhi remained diligent and hardworking, continuing to build his wealth. His son, Li Menhuan, grew up to be a studious young scholar who attained the highest ranking in the imperial examinations. He lifted the House of Li to ever greater heights. The man once scorned by his father-in-law as a poor man not truly worthy of his daughter's hand in marriage, gave to this very same woman a life of ease and riches. He brought great honor even to his already well-regarded in-laws, who had once thought him to be so lowly. Through a fortunate combination of hard work and great luck, Li Buzhi became one of the richest and most famous men in all Taiwan.

Questions for Discussion

1. Is it important for a person to marry someone whose family has a similar amount of money as does one's own family? Discuss why this should or should not be a factor in choosing a husband or wife.

2. Do you think that Yu Zhi and Li Buzhi could have been just as happy if the black gold bricks had remained unknown to them? Explain.

3. Did Li Menhuan have a more successful life because his father had discovered the rare black gold bricks? Could he have achieved success in his studies and profession anyway?

Suggestions for Class Activities

1. Have students research the origin and meaning of their names. Have them list notable people from the past or present who share this name, then choose one of these individuals and write a biographical sketch of her or him.

2. As indicated in the story, people on Taiwan choose the names of their children only after the first month. Have students investigate the naming traditions of other societies, such as those in Spain, Nigeria, and India, and then compare these traditions to the way in which the students were given their names.

Three

Have you ever had an experience that significantly changed the way you be-haved from that time forward? Here is a tale of how this happened to one of three brothers.

A Tale of Three Brothers

In days of old, there lived three brothers in a village of northern Taiwan. The oldest and the youngest of these brothers were good and kind, but the middle brother was a greedy sort of person.

One day these three brothers went on a trip to the district capital. Along the way, they stopped to rest beneath a tree. All of a sudden, seemingly out of nowhere, there appeared three jugs. When the brothers looked inside the jugs, they found all three full of silver and gold. All three brothers were of course elated. The older and younger brother felt that their good fortune was Heaven's reward for their kind ways and hardworking natures. The middle brother thought that if so much silver and gold was wonderful, more of such treasure would be even better. His mind was full of thoughts as to how he could turn good luck into better luck. After discussing matters awhile, the three brothers decided to leave the three jugs hidden in a pile of straw near the tree. They would retrieve their treasure on the way back home from the district capital.

The brothers traveled on together to the district capital. But the middle brother could think only of retrieving that treasure of silver and gold. He began to feign deep discomfort, screaming that his stomach hurt something awful. He complained to his brothers, "Oh, I'm just not up to this trip anymore. I've never had such a stomachache! But, please, don't worry. I'll be all right after I have a chance to rest quietly at home. You two don't have to wait for me. Just go on ahead, and I'll go back home to take some medicine and relax."

This middle brother then made haste back to the tree and searched in the straw for the three jugs. He found the jugs—but did he have a surprise coming! The silver and gold that had previously filled the two jugs had become something entirely different. The fine shine of the precious metals now had the murky appearance of very foul, smelly water. Disgusted and now really feeling that stomachache that he had faked before, the middle brother trudged home in great discontent.

But when his brothers returned to the tree on their way back from the district capital, they found the three jugs where they had left them, still full of silver and gold. These two brothers each took one jug in hand and helped each other carry the remaining jug. Once home, they said, they would divide the treasure according to a sensible plan: Because each jug held the same amount of silver and gold, each brother would take one jug.

Upon the return of his brothers, the middle brother lay on his bed, still feigning illness. When he saw that the jugs his brothers carried somehow now held silver and gold once again, his heart filled anew with greed. How he longed to have all of that treasure to himself! What was this awful trick that the three jugs had played on him? Then his heart did a flip when he heard his elder brother's words:

"Here, my brother, is your jug full of silver and gold. Younger brother and I certainly hope that you are feeling better. We know that wealth is nothing compared to health, but when you're feeling well again, we know that you will enjoy this fortune that the three of us found together."

Of course. His kind and honest brothers had returned to give him his one-third share of the treasure. The middle brother's heart emptied its greed as guilt poured in. But that guilt led to a new outlook on life. From that day forward, the middle brother changed his greedy ways. Love and generosity filled his soul, driving out the selfishness that had brought never-ending desire. Never again did he seek more than his share of life's bounty, and in fact from that day forward he tried to give more of himself and what he had to others than they returned to him. So it was that the generosity of his brothers, and their unselfish treatment of him, pointed his life in a new direction, showing him the way to a new life as a good and selfless man.

Questions for Discussion

1. What experiences have you had that changed the way you behaved or the way that you thought about something?

2. Why exactly did the middle brother of the story come to feel guilty about trying to take all of the treasure for himself? Do you think that he would have eventually come to feel guilty anyway?

3. Does being the first, second, or last born in a family make siblings behave differently? Think of examples of people you know as you answer this question. Explain any differences or similarities that you see in the pattern of sibling behavior.

Suggestions for Class Activities

1. Review examples from the literature of psychology on the subject of birth order. Present the class with theories and generalized findings of psychologists on common traits of firstborn, middle, and youngest children. Hold a class discussion in which students share personal examples (in the manner of discussion question 3) and explain whether general findings of psychologists seem to hold in the particular cases that the students describe.

2. Have the students write individual essays based on answers to discussion question number 1, explaining how some particular experience changed the way that they behaved or thought.

3. Have students write a different version of the story, based on the premise of discussion question number 2.

Four

What are the consequences for betraying the trust that another may place in us? Here is a story that explains how many Taiwanese feel about the betrayal of trust and the consequences of betrayal.

Justice Comes to Elder Sister Lintou

Many, many years ago, the land along the train station in the old capital city of Tainan was uncultivated forest, and in this woodland there grew a tree known as Lintou. In those days, there was a woman who married a businessman from the Quanzhou district of Fujian Province on mainland China. They had not been married long when one day the businessman told his wife that he had to return to his native village. He felt an obligation, he said, to offer sacrifices to his ancestors, and at the same time he would take care of a few commercial transactions. Saying that he would need a sizable amount of money, he asked his wife to provide him with the funds that he needed. His trusting wife thereupon gave him all of the money that she had in the world. And at the moment of their parting, the good woman simply told her husband to be very careful and to come back to her as soon as possible after taking care of his business.

How was she to know that, once gone, her untrustworthy husband would not return but would take another wife in Quanzhou? In those days, such news passed back and forth across the Taiwan strait along with the immigrants who came from Quanzhou to make a new life on Taiwan. News also traveled with those from Taiwan who would return, as had the young woman's husband, to Quanzhou and other places to give proper sacrifices in their ancestral villages. But most of these people did what the unfortunate wife's husband did not: They came back once again to Taiwan and to their families who loved them.

The young wife was so distraught over her husband's inconstancy that life became too much to bear. Though it is a terrible thing in Taiwanese culture to harm one's own body, the young woman saw no way of relieving her depression except through suicide. After her death, her vengeful spirit refused to disperse. It appeared frequently in the dark of night. A small-time peddler of those delicious rice tamales know as *zhongzi* found paper money used for offerings to the dead among his pile of money. Another person heard the plaintive cries of a wandering ghost every night after the woman's terrible act of suicide. So those who lived in the area were very fearful, hanging close to their homes in the ever-deepening darkness of the hours after sunset. This ghost came to be known as "Elder Sister Lintou" to the villagers and rural folk near the old capital.

In time, people of the area erected a temple in Elder Sister Lintou's honor, and for the worship of her wandering ghost. By providing shelter to the the restless ghost, these people hoped that Elder Sister Lintou would stop bothering people by making strange noises and doing mysterious things. They hoped that the ghost would be at peace and turn away from all ill deeds directed toward the living.

It is said that Elder Sister Lintou's spirit later found a good-hearted person of Quanzhou to transport her on one of those journeys back to Fujian Province in mainland China. Once on the mainland, Elder Sister Lintou made her way to the ancestral village of her husband. She found the no-good, conniving man living with a new wife and the children produced by this marriage. Elder Sister Lintou held no ill will toward these innocent ones of the man's new family, and she never bothered them as long as they lived. But the ghost of Elder Sister Lintou made sure that her unfaithful husband's life from this day forward was full of strange occurrences. The man never rested well at night, nor did he feel any peace during his daytime hours. And at his passing, the man's soul went on its own restless journey, destined to wander in the netherworld that holds none of the joys of Heaven or Earth.

Questions for Discussion

1. Why do you think that the husband of this story returned to Quanzhou? Can you come up with clues from what you know about the history of Taiwan?

2. Does it take a restless ghost to make a person feel haunted about a bad decision? Is it possible to feel haunted in this way without actually seeing a ghost?

3. What Taiwanese beliefs and values are evident in this story? How are these similar to, and different from, beliefs and values that you yourself have?

Suggestions for Class Activities

1. Have the students investigate the origin and development of beliefs in ghosts in Chinese societies, as well as such beliefs in European and Native American societies. Have students then give an oral report comparing and contrasting these beliefs.

2. Immigrants from Quanzhou and Zhangzhou adapted to the unique circumstances of life on Taiwan, but they also held on to certain traditions from the mainland. Have students identify customs they may still follow that originated in the place of their ancestry. Students may, for example, investigate the nature of customs surrounding birth, childrearing, marriage ceremonies, choice of residence (close to husband's family, mother's family, or neither), and funeral rituals. Have them illustrate these customs through charts, drawings, paintings, or some other visual presentation.

3. Have students locate Quanzhou and Zhangzhou on the map. By what method did people get to Taiwan from these places so long ago? How long did it take? Conduct research in the library or on the Internet to see what you can find out to share with the class.

Five

What happens when a person does not know how much is enough? The following story suggests how many Taiwanese would answer this question.

The Magical Rice Pot of Fairy Cave

In days of old, the city of Keelong had a place called Fairy Cave. Inside the cave, there was a *miaozhu,* or "keeper of the incense," who was a most fortunate man indeed. For atop the cave itself there was an opening through which each day flowed grains of rice. When the faithful came to burn incense in the temple, the flow of rice increased many times. The worshipers, and all of those who lived or traveled in the area, considered this to be a most curious and wondrous circumstance.

One day there came to the temple a merchant who had previously known nothing of the magic associated with Fairy Cave. When the man saw rice flow through the opening in the cave, the man felt this to be very strange, but he also saw in the mystery an opportunity for profit. In such a frame of mind, he said to the *miaozhu,* "My, all of that rice flowing through the crack must give you a great deal of the precious grain. I would love to buy your extra rice. But think about this: Since rice flows through the crack atop the cave every day, there must be hordes of rice stashed away. If the crack were widened a bit, wouldn't more rice flow? And wouldn't one who could sell such quantities become a person of wealth and fame? If you decide to try this, let me know. I would give you a good price for all of that rice and would make a fine profit for myself selling it for export."

At first the *miaozhu* didn't take the man's words to heart. But the keeper of the cave spent many hours alone in the cave, with plenty of time to think. When he thought of an even more abundant flow of rice spilling into the cave every day, his heart became greedy. A greedy heart gives in easily to temptation. The *miaozhu* grabbed a hoe and widened the opening. In so doing, he thought with great expectation, "Any moment now, even more rice will flow through the opening."

Sure enough, more rice than had ever flowed into Fairy Cave at one time began to come through the opening. The rice flowed on and on, fulfilling the greatest hopes of the *miaozhu*. But alas, who would have thought that after this one great avalanche of rice, not a single grain would ever flow through the opening again? By the time the merchant came calling again, the flow of rice had ceased. The *miaozhu* had no rice to sell. He now did not even have enough rice to feed himself.

And so the *miaozhu* lived out his days in deep regret. So spare did his existence become that he wasted away to nothing. His days on earth did not last long after his greed had stopped the flow of rice into Fairy Cave.

This crack in Fairy Cave is what people today call "White Rice Pot." So calling the crack atop the cave, people remember a magical past when rice flowed abundantly. But they know, too, that greed has forever taken the rice and the magic that once graced Fairy Cave.

Questions for Discussion

1. Should the keeper of the cave have known that following the merchant's suggestion to widen the cave opening would lead to trouble? Explain why you think that he should have foreseen this, or why you think that he could not have predicted the consequences.

2. What are some names of caves that you know? Tell what you know about how these caves got their names.

Suggestions for Class Activities

1. Show students some examples of Taiwanese art, particularly those made in panels or on scrolls. Have each student draw or paint a four-part panel illustrating (1) the magic of Fairy Cave before the *miaozhu* took the advice of the merchant, (2) the scene at the time the rice started flowing more abundantly, (3) the *miaozhu's* life after the rice ceased to flow, and (4) how Fairy Cave and the "White Rice Pot" might look today.

2. Have each student write a story about an imaginary cave and how it got its name.

3. Have students research caves and caving and share their findings with the class. Are there any caves in your area? If so, consider inviting a guest speaker—perhaps a forest ranger or scientist who works in the caves—to come to your class. What causes caves to form? Scientists today sometimes perform research in caves. What type of research is being done? Why? For what are they looking?

Six

How important is it to be kind to other people? Does such kindness usually have unforeseen benefits? This tale offers some answers to those questions.

The Fate of a Kind-Hearted Servant Girl

In olden days there was a servant girl named Jinye, a person whose heart was full of kindness. One day she was planting vegetables in the garden at the back of her master's house when there suddenly appeared a beggar so torn of garment and smelly of body as to offend even the most merciful Bodhisattva. In pitiful voice did the unseemly stranger beg of Jinye, "Oh, please, ma'am, give me a crust of something to eat. It has been so long since I have had even a tiny morsel of something in my stomach." Jinye gave the beggar a bowl of rice while satisfying her own hunger with a humble dish of potatoes.

Next day Jinye was outside washing her master's clothes when again the beggar came along. The mistress of the house was outside with Jinye, enjoying herself in the day's pleasant sunshine. The mistress had none of Jinye's kindheartedness, none of her servant girl's gentleness with fellow human beings. When again the beggar asked for some morsel of food, the mistress intervened. She gave the unfortunate man a nasty knock on the head and shooed him away. This was difficult for the sweet Jinye to bear. As the sun grew hotter and her mistress retreated into her fine mansion, Jinye seized the chance to scamper off in search of the beggar. She found him sprawled, famished and exhausted, beside a chattering stream. Jinye spoke softly to the forlorn man, "Wait here, sir. I'll be back soon with something to quiet your hunger." With that, Jinye stole back into the kitchen of her mistress. Tossing a few vegetables into a bowl of steaming rice, she hurried out of the mansion and ran all the way back to the stream.

A number of days went by when the mistress ordered Jinye to go down to the well-stocked pond on the property of the great landowner to catch a few shrimp. Jinye stood at pond's edge a long time but managed to catch not a single shrimp. She dreaded the beating and scolding that she knew awaited her back at the big house. In that instant of disquiet, she suddenly noticed the beggar, appearing now for the third time, having sat upon a boulder. He spoke thus to Jinye: "Would you be so kind as to help me lance this terrible boil that has long infected my poor foot?"

Such was the kindness of Jinye that she nodded her head and honored his request, assisting the beggar in lancing his boil. Some of the pus from the lanced boil splattered on Jinye's face, but she waited until the beggar had departed before going to the stream to wash her face. Then, when she pulled up her barrel to make the return journey home, Jinye discovered that it was full of shrimp. "Now, how did all of these shrimp fill my barrel so quickly?" Jinye spoke, as if asking the pond. "Catching shrimp in a stocked pond should not be so very difficult, and yet my luck has been so terrible all day until now." Very puzzled, she turned to make the trip home.

When Jinye got back to the mansion, her mistress yelled at her, "What in the world have you been up to? Hey, let me look at you! I can't believe what I'm seeing! What in the world is this all about?" Jinye's mistress held a mirror before the servant girl's face and said, "Just look at yourself. You've always been such an ugly little thing. How is it that your face has become a thing of beauty?"

For a few moments, Jinye was as surprised as her mistress. Then she thought of the beggar, the boil, and the pus that had splattered upon her face. As odd as it seemed, there must have been some connection between that disgusting liquid and the splendid transformation that had given her a radiantly beautiful face. In time, Jinye gave this interpretation of events to her mistress and braced for a scolding. But the mistress was too busy with thoughts of herself to strike out with words or blows against Jinye. Instead, the mistress said to her servant girl, "I want such a face myself. And since I will be starting out so very much more beautiful than did you, I may well be the world's most beautiful woman when the magic has been worked. I order you to make sure that what happened to your face now happens to my own!"

The next day, the beggar came again to the great house. Fresh boils dotted his gnarled feet. This time the mistress did not send the beggar rudely away. To the contrary, she took hold of him and braced herself for the terrible odor that she knew would be coming her way. With a heavy pinch upon the biggest boil, the mistress of the great house forced some of the pus from the poor man's burst boil onto her own face. With great excitement and expectation, she then ran as quickly as she could to the pond's edge.

The mistress cupped her hand into the waters to wash her face. But as she did so, she saw the terrible unexpected consequences of her rash actions. She had been transformed into something quite wretched. Her face was hideous, and feathers now covered her entire body.

At this point the beggar came into her sight. The mistress-turned-feathered creature saw the beggar walk straight toward Jinye, take her arm, and lead her away from the yard where her mistress had scolded her so often. As they walked away, the once-proud gentlewoman desperately yelled, "Someone, help! Oh please help me! My beautiful face is ruined! Oh, please, someone, help!"

But no one seemed to hear. The mistress of the fine mansion was alone in a physical wretchedness to match her unkind soul. Her face turned all the more hideous as she scrunched it up at the sight she saw. The mistress stared in helplessness as her now beautiful servant girl strolled out of the courtyard with a handsome man whose face bore no boils, no scars, no pain. He had become handsome, erect, sturdy, and tall—a fit companion for the girl whose kindness had given a new life to them both.

Questions for Discussion

1. What do you think explains the differing attitudes of Jinye and her mistress toward the beggar in this tale?

2. Do you think that kindness usually has unforeseen rewards? Do people have a right to expect such rewards, or is kindness its own reward?

Suggestions for Class Activities

1. Divide the class into groups of three people. Have the students in each of the groups choose one of the three main characters in the tale (Jinye, her mistress, or the beggar). Working in groups, have them take the tale and turn it into a play format, incorporating some of the dialogue as presented in the story but also creating some of their own.

2. After the students have written their plays, have the groups think about the props and set design that they will need to present them. Then have them rehearse and perform their plays in class. Set aside a special performance day and invite parents and others to come to school to see the various plays based on this Taiwanese tale. (A simpler version would be to have students write a readers theater script based on the tale, with a different group working on each episode. The students can then read their scripts in sequence.)

Seven

The Taiwanese have a very definite idea about how a young woman is sup-
posed to act toward her husband's family in general, and her mother-in-law in
particular. The young woman in this story relates to her mother-in-law in a way
that the Taiwanese feel deserves the very top level of respect.

The Virtuous Wife of Dajia

The town of Dajia in Taizhong County, Taiwan, is famous for two structures
that lie within its borders. One is Zhenluan Temple, dedicated to the goddess
Mazu. The other is a shrine dedicated to a woman named Lin Chunniang, a model
wife and mother-in-law.

During the reign of Emperor Jiaqing, a number of shrines to virtuous women
were erected throughout the territory controlled by the Qing dynasty. Such
shrines feature a stone arch, commemorating women who remained true to their
husbands even after their husbands had died. Such women never remarried, dedi-
cating themselves instead to the well-being of their mothers-in-law, their children, and all of those in the family of the deceased husband who needed
assistance. To honor such behavior and encourage it in others, people of the various regions would request imperial permission to build these stone arches, which
in time came to be known as *zhenjie fang,* or "Arches of Never-Failing Integrity."

Lin Chunniang of Taizhong's Dajia District came from a poor family. As
frequently happened under such circumstances, Lin Chunniang was sent to live
with another family in a neighboring village. Lin Chunniang, like so many others,
was betrothed to one of the boys in the family. She was raised with the under-
standing that she would assume the proper duties of a wife upon reaching
maturity.

Now this family, whose surname was Yu, had only one son, a young man
who traveled frequently around Taiwan on business. When Lin Chunniang was
only twelve years old, she received the news that her future husband had drowned
in a most unfortunate and unusual episode. Although the young girl was of such
tender years, she nevertheless resolved to remain a widow forever. This allowed
her to concentrate on the well-being of her elderly and ailing mother-in-law. The
lives of this older woman and Lin Chunniang came to be intimately intertwined.

The needs of Lin Chunniang's mother-in-law were great. Because the unfortunate woman had lost her only son, the most grievous loss that a Taiwanese mother can imagine, she cried day and night. Her sight was dimming in her elderly years, and the additional cover of her endless tears rendered her almost completely blind. The Yu family, though, had little money to call forth the services of a doctor. In the place of physicians, Lin Chunniang offered herself. She wiped her mother-in-law's tears away. She would then soothe the woman's eyes with a gentle sweep of her tongue. She also burned incense and offered prayers, greatly moving the Heavenly Emperor. Within six months, the older woman's eyes had been cured of their affliction.

Alas, though, the old woman soon developed another painful condition: severe cramping and twitching of her legs. And once again, Lin Chunniang dedicated herself to an effort to relieve the suffering of her mother-in-law. The ever-faithful daughter-in-law lifted and stretched the old limbs, caressing the frayed tendons. Lin Chunniang would also lovingly bathe her mother-in-law. Everything that she did was done in good cheer, with an absence of complaint. Her mother-in-law came to love and appreciate this daughter-in-law with an affection that knew no bounds.

When the old woman passed from this earth, Lin Chunniang suffered terribly. She busied herself with weaving in an effort to raise a bit of money, which she saved for the rearing of a young boy of the extended family Yu. The boy, who bore the name of Yu Zhixiang, was the son of a young man who had contracted an illness that brought him an early and untimely death. Distraught but determined to press on with her duties, Lin Chunniang helped his widow raise the child that the young man's death had left fatherless. Admiration for this extremely dedicated woman increased in proportion with her accumulation of good deeds.

The powerful story of Lin Chunniang extended far beyond the bonds of her own lifetime. In time, word of her exemplary behavior reached Huang Kaiji, the magistrate stationed in Tamsui, whose jurisdiction reached to the district of Dajia. Exceedingly touched by the tenor of Lin Chunniang's life, this magistrate submitted a memorial to Emperor Jiaqing, asking that a stone arch be erected in her honor. An ancestral tablet was placed in the shrine, so that Lin's spirit might be worshiped by all of those who wished to express their reverence for Lin Chunniang and for all of those cherished virtues for which her life was held to be a shining example.

Questions for Discussion

1. For what reasons do you think traditional Taiwanese society praised women who did not remarry after their husbands died? Think of all the reasons that you can and hold a thorough class discussion on this topic.

2. Women in today's Taiwan do not feel bound by all of the customs from the past. Many Taiwanese women today would, in fact, remarry if their husbands died. Do you think that going against this particular traditional expectation is likely to have good or bad effects for society as a whole? Explain.

3. Are there memorials or other markers or ceremonies of public recognition for people who have served your community well? Have students share their responses.

Suggestions for Class Activities

1. Have students think about people who deserve to be recognized by the community. Have them draw a design for a plaque, the contents of a mural, the form of a statue, or some other physical object honoring the person the class has chosen. Have them decide at what forum or in what manner the item should be presented to the honoree. Share illustrations and ideas with the class. An extension of this project might include deciding as a class to present one of these awards to a community member.

2. Divide students into groups of three or four, and then assign each group one historical period in U.S. women's history: 1848 (the year of the Seneca Falls Convention) through 1920 (the year that the Nineteenth Amendment to the United States Constitution went into effect), 1920–1973 (the year that Title IX went into effect), and 1973–2003 (the era during which women have become prominent in business and the professions). Have the students share their research findings with the class, using this as an opportunity to discuss and share opinions on gender roles. An excellent resource for this project is Sue Heinemann's *Amazing Women in American History: A Book of Answers for Kids* (New York: Stonesong/John Wiley and Sons, 1998).

3. Research traditional Taiwanese marriage and family customs. Are Taiwanese families *matriarchal* or *patriarchal*? Does this to some extent explain Lin Chunniang's devotion? When do you think this story took place? When did marriage and family customs begin to change in Taiwan? Why?

Part Two

Taiwanese Religion and Ethics

Eight

Have you ever known two friends whose lives took them down very different paths? Here is a story that tells the tale of two such friends.

The Friendship of Taiyang Pian and Zhi Wuye

Once there were a couple of beggars, one named Taiyang Pian, the other named Zhi Wuye. The two beggars bore a striking physical resemblance to each other, and they had become fast friends virtually from the moment they entered the world. Their births were scarcely fifteen minutes apart, and their families lived next door to each other. Their life circumstances were also similar. Their families were poor and had many children. The two friends left their villages together on their wandering course when they were only sixteen years old, forced to find a way to survive when their families could no longer provide for them.

One day these two good friends sat talking about their future. They agreed that a lifetime spent begging others for the necessities of life would be a waste. They ultimately decided that they would part company for a while, hoping to find their ways to better fortune. And so it was that they took leave of each other, one traveling east, and the other west.

Taiyang Pian took the eastern route, coming in time to a city that he had never visited before. Exhausted from his daylong journey, he ensconced himself rather absentmindedly at the finely carved front door of a wealthy family's house to take his nightly rest. There lived in this home a beautiful young woman who had conspired with her beloved to steal away from home and village. In the middle of the night, the young woman tied her gold and silver coins along with articles of clothing into a cloth bundle. She then lowered the bundle from her upstairs window. As it happened, these landed on the head of the sleeping Taiyang Pian. In a dream-muddled state, the beggar took the bundle with a skillful motion and placed it under his head for a pillow. After a while, the young woman also lowered a sheet and slid down from her window only to find the snoozing beggar rather than the loved one for whom she had been waiting. Her beloved was nowhere in sight. Seeing that the beggar was using her bundle as a pillow and continuing to scan the distance for a sign of her beloved, the young woman was seized with a deep sadness. She was very confused as to what to do.

The young woman waited and waited. She saw no trace of her loved one as the night wore on. The night was still and quiet. She heard little except the soft snores of the soundly sleeping Taiyang Pian. At last she concluded that her beloved had backed out of their decision to elope. Remaining at home and going about her usual schedule would keep her too close to all of the places, reminding her of all of the times, that she and her love had shared. She made a snap decision to go with this beggar on his rambles. As the first sign of light shone in the eastern sky, the young woman spoke to her uninvited guest: "I can tell from your clothes and the way that you have settled yourself here to sleep that you are a wandering beggar. I want to go with you on your travels."

Taiyang Pian heard this request in a kind of fog brought on by deep slumber. Before too long, though, his head cleared and his mind was fresh as he responded in the way that he knew he must. He could tell that this deeply sad and hurt young woman needed a friend and that she needed to get away from those things that had caused the pain. He answered her not with words from his mouth, but rather with the look upon his face and the movement of his body. Tai Yangpian simply took the young woman's arm and led her gently out of her village and onto the roadway that for so long had been his home.

The two strolled for a long while, from dawn to dusk, over hills, through valleys, and across the plains of the Taiwanese countryside. In time, they came to the home of a wealthy family, where they asked to take a night's rest. The head of the house wore a kind expression on his face, though at first he was not encouraging. "I'm so very sorry," he said, "but just a while ago other visitors claimed the last of our spare rooms and beds. I do, though, have another house that my family never uses. It is on some additional property that I bought not long ago. It is a nice enough house, though we've never had occasion to stay there. It is just down the road about a half a mile, and you are welcome to stay there for the night."

Then the landowner spoke some less soothing words: "I must tell you of one complication. Though I have never witnessed it myself, a number of people say that a ghost appears inside the house at nightfall. I leave the house unlocked, and one might have thought that beggars and other weary travelers would have sought the house out. But to my knowledge, no one has dared to stay in the house since a mysterious death in the family of the original owner."

What were the beggar and the young woman to do? They had no other place to rest their weary feet or lay their leaden heads. They decided that they had better brave a night in the house, even if many thought it was haunted. They walked down the road, strolled into the courtyard, and warily pushed open the front door. The two travelers settled in for their night's slumber, and for a long while, they rested well. But sure enough, as the darkness of night reached its greatest intensity, not one but two ghosts appeared. Both ghosts were hideous and fierce of face. One was red, the other green. The beggar and the young woman felt fear such as they had never before known. They felt as though their own souls had been separated from their bodies, especially as the red-faced ghost spoke to them in a frightful tone: "What took you so long? We've been waiting for the two of you for many years."

Taiyang Pian trembled, and his voice shook and cracked as he spoke: "Waiting for us? We've only known each other a short time. How could you have known that we were coming?"

"You must surely have seen us before," said the green-faced ghost. We usually can be found guarding the shrines to Tudi Gong, the protector of villages and land. You must have seen us guarding the entrance to these shrines. We know a great many things that people do not."

Next the red-faced ghost spoke again. Its voice remained deep and impressive, but its message was anything but frightful: "Below the floor," the ghost explained, "lies chest upon chest of gold and silver, all of which is yours for the taking. We've been protecting these valuables for the two of you for lo these many burdensome years."

Now the young woman mustered the courage to speak. She began, "But how—"

Before she could continue, the two ghosts had vanished. After puzzling over what all of this might mean, Taiyang Pian and the young woman fell into a deep sleep from sheer exhaustion.

As dawn broke on a cool morning, Taiyang Pian went to see the landowner who had offered this house to them for the night. He offered the surprising news that he wanted to purchase the house and a bit of the land around it.

"I never really wanted that house anyway," said the owner. "If you really want to buy it, just give me whatever money you can, and it's yours."

Taiyang Pian was able to give the magistrate some of the money that the young woman had brought along. He then returned to his newly purchased house to dig for much greater treasure. He dug and dug, then after many hours of effort he found what the divine officials sent from the heavens by Tudi Gong had promised. There was indeed a great abundance of gold and silver lying in trunks deep beneath the floor. This treasure proved enough to ensure a life of wealth and ease for this man who had been a mere beggar, and for the young woman whose beloved had proven so unfaithful. Having grown very fond of each other, and convinced that their good fortune was the result of the circumstances that had brought them together, Taiyang Pian and the young woman decided that they were fated to be husband and wife. They married in a great ceremony attended by everyone in their new city of residence.

The two former wanderers settled into their new house. It was a well-built and spacious home. Soon their clothes and manner of life took on the styles of the finest landowning families. Before too very long, Taiyang Pian and his young bride were recognized as the wealthiest and most influential people in the city. They had everything that Taiwan and the whole wide world could offer in material comfort to make them happy. But inside Taiyang Pian's heart, there was a severe emptiness that neither newfound love nor gold and silver could fill.

He moped around every day, all day long. From the moment that he and Zhi Wuye had parted, Taiyang Pian had begun to miss his friend terribly. When he thought of the days when he and Zhi Wuye had divided the food that they had begged, and when he thought of the days—good and bad—that they had shared, and the fact that he alone of the two former beggars now enjoyed such bounty, he felt guilty. He felt as though he had done Zhi Wuye some great injustice. He began to give generously to beggars and all the poor people who came to his attention, and he tried everything he knew to locate his friend Zhi Wuye. He sent letters far and wide to people known by those in his now-wide circle of influential friends. But for the longest time, no sign came of Zhi Wuye, not the slightest hint of where the travels of this old and dear friend had led.

One day beggars and poor people from many different places crowded around the big front door of the grand house that Taiyang Pian shared with his wife. Taiyang Pian opened that big door to bestow personally the generous amount of food that he offered as his daily gift to those in need. But though those at his door were many, and he distributed food late into the evening, he saw no trace of his long-lost friend. Then, just as he was about to shut the door in disappointment, another beggar stumbled forward. It was none other than the man with whom friendship had been formed in poverty and hardship, the friend he had never forgotten, his dear companion of old: Zhi Wuye.

Taiyang Pian helped his friend into the parlor, gave him time to enjoy a warm bath and change into brand new clothes. And yet Zhi Wuye could not enjoy these. He felt as if the crisp new clothes pierced his body like a sharp pin. As if to relieve himself from suffering, Zhi Wuye tore the new garments from his body and donned his old, tattered clothes. He said to a disappointed Taiyang Pian, "I'm sorry, dear friend, but I must be on my way. It seems that the beggar's life is the life for me, after all."

You see, Zhi Wuye felt deeply that it was his fate to be a beggar, no less than it had been Taiyang Pian's fate to find great treasure and marry a beautiful woman. Taiyang Pian pleaded with his old friend to stay, but Zhi Wuye had made up his mind. Seeing that there was nothing that he could do to persuade his friend to stay, Taiyang Pian saw no other course but cheerfully to bid Zhi Wuye to go in freedom. He wanted to give him some money to help him along his journey, but he knew that his friend would not accept more from him than was necessary to fulfill the needs of the immediate moment. Then he thought of a plan. Taiyang Pian placed several pieces of gold and silver inside a portion of Taiwanese bread known as Turtle Buns, which he then gave to his friend.

After Zhi Wuye departed, he met up with his beggar companions, trodding the same familiar roads. He was able to exchange some of the bread that Taiyang Pian had given him for a few of the potatoes that his friends had managed to get. He bartered away all but one piece of bread. Only as he bit into the bread did he realize that Taiyang Pian had placed eight silver pieces inside every bun.

Zhi Wuye thought fondly of his old friend, but he had no impulse to go back to the house where gold and silver were commonplace. Seven of those silver pieces bought a great many useful items for Zhi Wuye and his companions for many, many months. The eighth one he never spent at all. He had a hole drilled in that coin, then he ran a string through it so that he could wear it around his neck. Zhi Wuye never returned to see the friend who now was living such a different life. But he kept the coin close to his heart. The coin necklace was a constant re-minder to Zhi Wuye of a faithful companion and the different fates that may come even to those who begin life's journey together.

Questions for Class Discussion

1. Have you ever seen or heard of a haunted house? What kind of stories did you hear about it? Did you believe them? Why or why not? Would you have been able to spend the night in a house that many people said was haunted, as did Taiyang Pian and the young woman in this story?

2. What are the characteristics of a good friend? Are you such a friend to somebody?

Suggestions for Class Activities

1. Have the students design their own symbols for friendship and illustrate the symbols in a drawing or painting. Have students show their own designs and explain how the symbols illustrate friendship. As a class, discuss how symbols might be used, for example, in jewelry, on note cards and stationary, or on clothing. You may wish to undertake a class design project using these symbols.

2. Read three stories from classic or quality contemporary American literature (selecting them from culturally diverse sources) that present images of friendship. After the reading, have a class discussion about what each of these stories tells us about friendship, then have students write a poem or essay on the topic, "A Friend is . . ."

3. Conduct research in the library or on the Internet to find Taiwanese or other Asian depictions of ghosts. Compare and contrast these to Western ghosts.

Nine

One of the most important values in Taiwanese society is the idea of "filial piety," the respectful behavior that is due to one's parents and other family elders. Here is a tale that deals with this theme and one of the symbols used by the Taiwanese to express their respect for ancestors.

The Origins of the Taiwanese Ancestral Tablet

Once upon a time there was a farmer named Ding Lan, who was both unfilial [neglectful of one's duties, or demonstrating disrespectful behavior, toward a parent] and bad-tempered. Every day his mother tried to please him with the lunch that she sent to him in the fields, but pleasing Ding Lan was difficult to do. If she sent it to him early, Ding Lan would complain that she had sent it too soon. If she sent it later, he would gripe that she had sent it too late. It didn't matter when she sent his lunch to him—Ding Lan seemed to enjoy complaining more than anything. His mother suffered from his constant scolding and passed her days in great sadness.

One very early morning, Ding Lan went with his hoe into the fields as usual. Along the way, he saw a ewe that had just given birth. As soon as the lamb appeared, it kneeled before its mother and did not move, as if it were worshiping her with most sincere devotion. Puzzled, Ding Lan asked an elderly man who happened to pass by, "Say, see that lamb over there? What is it doing?"

The man replied, "First of all, do you always address your elders with 'Say'? Is it not more proper to address a person of my years as 'Honorable One'? You might find an answer to your question regarding the lamb's behavior in the correct answer to that question."

The old man continued, "The greatest thing on earth is a mother's love. In order that you might develop properly in life, she assumes the burden of pregnancy, bearing you those nine long months. She then takes on the many duties of nurturing you through your young life. Not only does the human mother do this; the beasts of the field and forest do the same. Look at that lamb! As soon as it was born, it thanked its mother for her labor. The first thing that it did was to kneel before her reverently."

Hearing these words from the elder, Ding Lan was very moved. He felt so very ashamed. Not only had he failed to express his appreciation to his mother for all that she had labored to do for him. He had also exhibited the worst sort of temper in his mother's presence, wounding her heart every day with his constant scolding. As he continued to make his way to the field, Ding Lan saw a pair of mother birds fussing over their nests. Each bird held a little worm gripped in its beak. Each mother bird was feeding a young bird lying small and vulnerable in its nest. This additional sign of motherly devotion deepened Ding Lan's guilt. Sadness and regret built up inside of him, overwhelming his unsettled soul.

The next day, Ding Lan's mother had business to attend to and could not send him his meal on time. She feared that the usual scolding would be all the greater if she did not send her son some kind of meal. Ding Lan's mother approached her son as if she were risking her life. Ding Lan could see his mother approaching from afar, bearing her load with great difficulty. He suddenly dropped his hoe and went forward to greet her. His mother had never seen Ding Lan run toward her in this manner. She could not in her wildest dreams imagine that he would do so. Ding Lan's mother was so taken aback that she put her basket down and began running away from her son. She looked back frequently and took scarce notice of where she was going. In her haste and carelessness, she came at one instance upon a pond and, before she could stop herself, fell into the waters. Unable to swim, all that she could do was to thrash about in the pond helplessly. From too far away, Ding Lan could see what had happened, and he quickened his pace all the more. But he was too late. He could not save his mother. She sank before his very eyes.

Desperately, Ding Lan dove into the pond and went down and down again repeatedly in search of his mother. But her body disappeared mysteriously. At one point, Ding Lan hoped against hope as his hands brought forth some solid item. It was a wooden plank. For some reason, Ding Lan could not let go of this object. He clung to it when at last he gave up and climbed back onto the shore of the pond.

With great sadness and a tortured soul, Ding Lan brought this wooden plank back to his house. At the top of it, he wrote his mother's name and placed it at the center of the altar table in the parlor, in company with the images of gods and holy items on display. From that time forward, people would use such a wooden plank as the ancestral tablet displayed in like manner at most Taiwanese homes. Formally known as the "Tablet of the Divine Master," one of its alternative names suggests its origins in the Ding Lan episode: "Tablet of the Honorable Mother." Taiwanese people place such tablets upon their altars to honor those ancestors whose labors made the existence of future generations possible.

Questions for Discussion

1. In Taiwan, China, and many other countries, showing respect to parents or elders is very important. Is it important in the United States? Do you think respect is deserved, or must it be earned? How do you show respect to your parents? How do you show respect to other adults?

2. Can you think of anything in U.S. society that is similar to the ancestral tablet of the Taiwanese? How do people in the United States show respect for people in their families who are no longer living? What kind of influence might an ancestor have on your life?

3. Taiwanese people think that one reason children should have respect for their parents is because parents do so many things for their children when they are young. What are the characteristics of a good parent? If you ever become a parent, what would you want to do for your children? What would you want to teach them?

Suggestions for Class Activities

1. Have each student compose a poem that tells the story of Ding Lan, the fate of his mother, and the creation of the Taiwanese ancestral tablet.

2. Have students create a family tree based on their own knowledge and on interviews with parents, grandparents, and other relatives. Students might choose one of their ancestors and write their life story.

Ten

Have you ever thought of nature's creatures as friends who might just offer you help when you need it most? The following story is a much-loved Taiwanese tale that demonstrates this idea:

A Heart Buzzing with Kindness

There once was a Taiwanese farmer by the name of Ah Fu, a very fine person admired for his kindness by everyone in his village. One day Ah Fu went into the city and saw a fortuneteller, an elderly woman whom he asked to foretell his fate in life.

The fortuneteller studied Ah Fu's face a while and then said, "Your body is extremely warm. It's very unlikely that you will live to see tomorrow morning."

When Ah Fu heard this, he was stunned to the bone. Turning to go, he thought, "I haven't done anything to offend Heaven or the principles of human-kind. What have I done to deserve such a fate?" Confused to the depths of his soul, he let out with an angry cry. The force of his cry, though, seemed to jerk him from his self-focused inner misery. He looked about and became more alert to what was going on around him.

Ah Fu's eyes lit on a little boy who held a torch in his hand. Three other boys stood around him. They were all staring in the same direction. The torch seemed to be the focus of their activity. Intrigued, Ah Fu came forward to inquire, "My little boys, what would you be doing playing with fire?"

The boys responded, "There's a beehive right ahead there, and we intend to burn it down."

Hearing this, Ah Fu urged them in his kindly, gentle manner, "Please do not harm the innocent bees at home in their hive. They have every bit as much right to live out the natural years of their lives as do you and I. I'll give each of you five coins if you refrain from burning down their beehive. Now take these, and go on your way."

The boys accepted gladly. When Ah Fu returned home, he lay down and tried to rest. But his thoughts immediately turned to the prediction of the old fortune-teller. In time, he decided that it was useless to try to sleep. He said to himself, "I really have so little time left on this Earth, why don't I spend my time doing something that I truly love to do? I think I'll relax in a good, hot bath."

With that, Ah Fu fired up the stove and boiled a big pot of water. He took a pail of the water into the bathroom and started to pour it into his tub. Just as he began to prepare his bath, he heard some high-pitched voices join together to warn him, "Ah Fu, be careful!" To Ah Fu's amazement, some force unseen in the dimly lit bathroom jerked the pail from his hands, then turned it so as to spill the hot liquid onto the floor.

"Aargh! Oh, ouch! I burn!" said some voice that Ah Fu could not locate exactly. At that moment, Ah Fu's wife heard the commotion and came running with lantern in hand. In the glow of the lantern, Ah Fu and his wife now saw a snake trapped and lifeless under the water pail. A thick cloud of bees buzzed nearby, drifted to a nearby window, then passed out into the fields just beyond Ah Fu's house.

Ah Fu had narrowly escaped being bitten by the deadly serpent. He thought for a moment and realized that his rescuers must be the very same bees that he himself had given new life when he paid the mischievous boys to be on their way. Ah Fu's kindness, and his new friends the bees had helped him escape the fate predicted by the fortuneteller.

In the days, weeks, and years to come, return visits to the fortuneteller always produced more favorable forecasts. The kindhearted Ah Fu lived out the full measure of his years with his wife and children, who in turn gave him the grandchildren who make the Taiwanese life complete.

Questions for Discussion

1. Would you have come to the defense of the bees as Ah Fu did in this story? Why or why not?

2. Why did the bees save Ah Fu from the snake? Have you ever returned kindness in this way? If so, share your story with the class.

3. Do you think that the good that people do usually comes back to them with some happy result later on? If this has ever happened to you, tell the class about it.

Suggestions for Class Activities

1. Create a mural that illustrates this story. Divide the class into groups, each responsible for creating a panel for a series of drawings that will illustrate the important phases of this story: the trip to the fortuneteller; Ah Fu's encounter with the naughty boys tormenting the bees; Ah Fu's look of surprise when he hears the mysterious voice in the dimly lit bathroom; Ah Fu's wife arriving with a lantern to reveal the snake under the pail and the bees buzzing away; scenes from Ah Fu's long, happy life in the years after this story occurs.

2. Take a trip to a nature preserve, or simply walk outside, stopping at certain points to discuss how certain plants and animals provide things beneficial to human beings. Discuss how human beings can better care for the natural world.

3. Have students research bees and write a report on them. Discuss types of bees, social structures, and how bees communicate with each other.

Eleven

Have you ever known someone who got away with some bad behavior for a long time before finally having to face punishment? Have you ever known a really good person who had to wait a long time to get the treatment that she or he deserved? Here is a story that the Taiwanese tell about just these sorts of situations.

A Wealthy Landowner, a River Spirit, a City God

In days of old, there was a very rich landowner in central Taiwan who each year took his great harvest to sell in the nearby city of Jiayi. On such occasions, he rode in a sedan chair carried on the shoulders of two of his servants. As the landlord rode homeward after selling his crops, the jingle-jangle of his new gold and silver made music pleasing to his ears.

On one of these trips home from the market town, the two attendants carrying the landowner's sedan chair hatched a secret plot to kill the wealthy man and make off with his treasure. They carried the sedan chair up a steep hill and paused as they neared the edge of a cliff. The two thieves dumped the sedan chair into the airy depths beneath the cliff and saw the landlord fall to his doom in the valley below.

Such a violent, early death is a great misfortune in the eyes of the Taiwanese people. Misfortune of this kind produces an angry ghost that forever seeks relief for its injured soul. In the aftermath of this particular incident, the landlord was transformed into a river spirit that passed its days lonely and adrift on the currents.

At the river's edge, there lived a fisher, a filial son who did his best to feed himself and his elderly parents. Every day he went to the river to fish, but few fish swam in the shallow part of the river near the shore. Out in the deeper sections, a dangerous undertow made it impossible to get to the more plentiful fish that swam there. So the number of fish that the filial son could provide for his parents was limited, and the three of them lived with a constant rumble in their bellies.

They were constantly hungry, that is, until one day the river spirit arose to say to the fisher, "Elder brother fisher, how would you like to be my sworn brother?"

"But aren't you a river spirit?" replied the fisher. "What would be the sense in the two of us becoming sworn brothers?"

"Oh," responded the river spirit, "there would be many advantages to your becoming my sworn brother! When you come to fish from now on, all you'll have to do is yell, 'My sworn brother, I've arrived!' Then I'll gather a big batch of fish, large ones and small ones, as many as you and your elderly parents need. You'll gain an easy catch, time after time. The three of you will never have to listen to the rumble of empty bellies again."

"Well, then, if you're not just saying all of this to pull some kind of trick on me, I will indeed become your sworn brother!"

Thereafter, just as the river spirit had promised, the fisher came away with a big catch every time he went to the river. The friendship between fisher and river spirit deepened with each passing day. They became as close as those sworn in brotherhood are supposed to become. Many years went by before that restlessness that generally dwells in those who have died violent deaths grew unbearable to the river spirit. One day, the spirit found itself saying to its sworn brother, "My brother! We must part ways tomorrow!"

"Oh, my, no," replied the startled fisher. "Why must you go?"

"I must follow another turn of the Wheel [reincarnation over multiple lifetimes] and live life as a human being once more," explained the river spirit.

"But how are you going to accomplish this?" asked the fisher.

"Well . . ." The spirit broke off, pausing for a moment before continuing. "That is, it's like this: Tomorrow about noon there will come a woman heading to town to sell her vegetables. She'll pause at river's edge here to rinse the vegetables. I'll grab her basket and fly away. She'll lunge toward me, trying to get her basket back. She'll drown in the attempt, and I'll be able to enter her body as it drifts toward the river bottom. Thus, my soul will be able to live in a human being once again."

As the fisher heard this, he began to tremble. His head felt light. His body seemed to break out with sweat at every pore.

"Now, you absolutely must not tell a single soul, my dear sworn brother," continued the river spirit. The river spirit repeated this warning three times.

The next day at noon the fisher was at river's edge when, according to the river spirit's prediction, a vegetable seller arrived to dip her basket of vegetables into the water. As the river spirit snatched her basket away, she moved as if to lunge for the basket. The kindhearted fisher could not help yelling out a warning, "Be careful! Do not go into that water! You'll drown!"

The vegetable seller obeyed the fisher's warning. Her life was spared. But because the plan had been foiled, the river spirit lost its chance to live again in the body of a human being: It could not at this time be reincarnated.

Before long, though, the river spirit came up with another plan for reincarnation. He once again told the fisher the plan and bade him refrain this time from letting the secret slip out. Next day at noon a newly married couple was going to pay the respects due from bride and groom to the family of the bride, bringing with them traditional rice cakes as a gift. Along the way, they would pause to give the rice basket a rinse in the river, and the river spirit would cause the currents to carry the basket away. When the young husband jumped into the river to retrieve the basket, he would be caught in the currents and drown. As that was happening, the river spirit would occupy the body and thus gain his opportunity for reincarnation.

And so it happened. As the basket drifted away, the young husband jumped into the river to retrieve the basket. The good-hearted fisher once again could not help yelling out a warning: "Get out! Get out of that river! You'll drown if you go any farther!" The young man got out of the river just in the nick of time, and once again the river spirit had lost its chance.

Months passed with the river spirit adrift on the currents. Then the King of the Underworld took pity on it. Having witnessed its loyalty and good deeds done on behalf of its sworn brother the fisher, and having seen its efforts to become human once more, the King of the Underworld offered another alternative. The King raised the river spirit to the status of City God, honored to sit in a fine temple erected in his honor in the city of Jiayi. And as for the City God's sworn brother, the kind-hearted fisher, the King of the Underworld invited him to visit the Crystal Palace where the King lived far under the sea. The King of the Underworld sent the fisher away from this visit laden with gold and other jewels.

As the fisher returned to land carrying the treasure given him by the King of the Underworld, he was attacked by two robbers. As it turned out, these were the same two who had killed the rich landholder and made off with his gold. Having squandered that wealth in reckless living, they now turned to thievery once more to get what they desired.

But the fisher was a good soul who had saved the lives of other human beings, and he was a sworn brother to the high-placed City God. The City God sensed that something was wrong with brother fisher. He sent forth his attendants to investigate, and the two robbers were brought before the City God.

The twists and turns of fate had brought the robbers to justice. Each robber clung stubbornly to a gold brick stolen from the fisher. But as they stood before the City God the bricks turned into mud. From this mud there dropped documents detailing their past deeds. Soon the sedan carriers-turned-robbers came to understand that they stood before the landowner, now a City God who would judge them for their deeds. Their knees began to tremble as they waited to hear the punishment they would receive.

Questions for Discussion

1. Why do some people steal? What are the consequences of stealing in our society? Do you think anything can prevent stealing or make it happen less often?

2. Do you think that crimes such as those committed by the robbers in this story are eventually punished, as was the case in this tale?

3. What punishment do you think the robbers in this story received from the City God? What punishment do you think would be appropriate?

Suggestions for Class Activities

1. Write a readers theater script based on this story, providing roles for all of the characters introduced in the tale. This is a multisession activity in which the teacher records lines spoken by the characters after thorough discussion by the students as to what dialogue should actually be included in the play. Have students take turns playing parts and being members of the audience. After everyone has had a chance to participate as an actor, you might choose a group to perform the play for a students in lower grades.

2. Stage a mock trial based on the final scene of this story in which the robbers come before the City God. Act out students' responses to discussion question three.

3. Have students draw a map of Taiwan that shows all of the rivers and bodies of water, as well as major cities.

Part Three

Taiwanese Tales of Natural Origins

Twelve

Have you ever watched fireflies flashing through a summer's night and wondered how these fascinating creatures came to be? The Taiwanese have a tale about the origin of fireflies that goes like this.

The Origin of Fireflies

Near the old Taiwanese capital city of Tainan, there once lived a farmer's wife who literally worked herself to death. Like so many Taiwanese people, she and her family had come to the island from the Chinese mainland province of Fujian, hoping to escape the poverty and hunger of their overcrowded region. Many did gain a better life on Taiwan, but not without continual struggles to produce rice and other crops on fertile soil forever challenged by hurricanes, floods, and pests. Weighed down by the responsibilities of cooking, cleaning, and raising her two children while working long days beside her husband in the fields, the weary wife's health began to worsen. Death took her while she was only in her forties, leaving her children to the care of her husband.

The two children were girls, the elder named Jingu and the younger Jinzhen. They grew up as bright as they were beautiful. Left without a mother, they drew very close to each other and loved each other dearly.

One summer evening after dinner, the two sisters sat outside the doorway of their home fanning themselves and delighting in the occasional gusts of a pleasant evening breeze as they waited for their father to return home from his late labor in the fields. At least they hoped that he would return that evening. The girls' father worked long days in the family fields. The plots were scattered and a long distance from home by foot. Often working late into the evening, he would take his slumber at the side of the rice paddy, waiting to return home until a good night's sleep revived his aching limbs.

Younger sister Jinzhen after a while thought of a playful challenge based on this doubt about their father's time of return. Who could guess correctly whether their father would return this evening? She thought that he would and in this belief said to elder sister Jingu, "Elder sister, let's see who can guess whether papa will come home from the fields this evening. See those three big bags of rice here near our doorway? I say that she who guesses incorrectly should have to move them to the storage shed all by herself. Will you play this game with me? What do you think? Will father come home this evening or not?"

Now as it happened, Jingu had made a special plea to her father early that same morning. He had for days labored so long and far away in the fields that every night he had left his daughters to put themselves to bed and took his night's rest on a mattress provided by nature. But that morning, Jingu had begged papa to come home to her and Jinzhen before bedtime, and he had promised her that he would.

Out of love and concern for her little sister, though, Jingu did not use this knowledge to gain the advantage in the contest suggested by Jinzhen. She worried that her sister was too small and weak to move the big sacks. And she knew Jinzhen was both stubborn and conscientious. If she lost the contest, she surely would try to move those heavy bags of rice all by herself, even if she strained her back doing so. Responding to her sister's challenge, Jingu replied: "Okay, I'll play. I say that father will not return until tomorrow morning."

"Good, because I think that he will return to us tonight and sleep in his own bed for the first time in a long time," said Jinzhen.

And so the girls waited at the doorway for a long time that evening. The sun set, and the intense tropical heat of southern Taiwan eased as darkness crept gradually over the land. Papa did not return. There must have been some unforeseen delay. Papa was not one to break his promises. Jinzhen grew downcast as bedtime neared. She had apparently lost the contest. Jingu tried to console her. "It's okay, little sister," she said. "I just got lucky. We can wait until father returns tomorrow morning. He can help us move those big bags. He wouldn't want you to move those all by yourself."

But sure enough, the stubborn Jinzhen replied, "No, a contest is a contest, and there must be a loser. I lost. According to my own rules, I must move the sacks."

"Well, then, at least let me help you, if you won't wait for father to return and help us," pleaded Jingu.

"No. That wasn't the deal. I lost, and I must move those bags tonight, all by myself," persisted Jinzhen.

Conscientious though Jinzhen was, she wasn't strong enough. She tried and tried but could not budge the heavy sacks. Embarrassed and frustrated, tears welled up in her eyes, and she ran away into the fields.

Jingu followed close behind her. She worried about her little sister being out all by herself late at night, especially in the mood that she was in. Jinzhen was so fast, though, that she got deep into the fields before Jingu could catch up with her. And Jinzhen had paid little attention to where she was going. She stood lost and lonely in the deepening darkness now taking over the hours after midnight.

When long after midnight elder sister Jingu still had caught no sight of Jinzhen, she became frantic about the safety of her little sister. She rushed everywhere she thought Jinzhen might be, determined to find her and bring her home. Disappointed at every turn, she refused to give in to hopelessness. She refused to give up. Yet at one point, exhausted with all of her scurrying about, she collapsed on the ground and yielded to her body's demand for rest. Even then, she used the time to think of a way to find her sister and bring her home.

"A lantern! If I only had a lantern!" Jingu longed for a kerosene-fueled light that would allow her to penetrate the darkness. Jingu's unshakable optimism told her that a lantern would light a path that would lead her to her precious little sister. But she had run so far that no farmhouse lay anywhere near. Where would she find a lantern within distance of these isolated fields? She had no answer. In time all she could do was to muster her courage and go on in the darkness, guided only by a sliver of a moon.

Tired to the bone, Jingu walked on. "Jinzhen! Where are you, little sister? Please hear me! Come out, if you're hiding! I am so worried, Jinzhen! Where are you, precious one?"

The only reply came from crickets and frogs at home in the dead of night amid field and stream. Jingu pressed on. She was very, very tired. In her fatigue, she became careless. At one point, not feeling her way with care in the deepening darkness, Jingu failed to see a large hole that plunged several feet below the surface of the fields. Jingu fell to a depth that proved too much of a challenge for her to escape. Her efforts to climb out got her nowhere. She was trapped, and by the time a search party found her, she had lost her life at an age even younger than had her unfortunate mother.

Or, more accurately, Jingu had lost the life of those whose bodies cling to bones, and under whose flesh warm blood runs its course. She passed into a ghostly state that seemed only a vague suggestion of the girl that she had been. But even in this ghostly, otherworldly form, Jingu continued the search for her little sister. Not knowing that Jinzhen had fared better than herself and had been rescued by her father on his way home at early morn, Jingu refused to give up the search that she thought still her responsibility. Now possessing a light that served as the lantern she had not been able to find in her crucial moment of need, she searched every field, thicket, and forest near Tainan. Then throughout Taiwan, across the seas, in many lands she continued the search. She lacked the cues and ability to reason that those in the former life possess, and so her search was wandering, doomed to disappointment. But she was relentless, determined, unyielding to failure at every turn. She found no Jinzhen, but her search went on. How would she ever find that beloved little sister? Whether she had success or not, she would never give up.

And we all have watched Jingu in this never-ending search for Jinzhen. For those insects flitting through the dark on a summer's late evening are what the Taiwanese call *huo jingu*: "Fire-bearing *jingu*," or "Girl of the Golden Flame." This is the firefly, the reincarnated Jingu of our story, flashing through the night in continual search for the little sister that she holds so dear.

Questions for Discussion

1. Do you think that Jingu was right to predict purposely the wrong time of her father's return? Explain.

2. Why did Jinzhen run away? Have you ever felt as Jinzhen did when she could not move the heavy sacks of rice?

3. What does the story of Jingu becoming a firefly say about her love for her little sister? For whom do you feel this sort of strong, powerful love?

Suggestions for Class Activities

1. Have each student write or tell a tale about her or his own experience with fireflies or create a story about the origins of fireflies. Follow up with an opportunity to illustrate the students' stories.

2. Investigate the biological facts about fireflies, or lightning bugs. In the course of their investigations, have the students seek answers to questions such as the following:

   • How long have fireflies existed?

   • What do fireflies eat?

   • How long do fireflies live?

   • How do fireflies reproduce?

   • What causes the light that one sees as the firefly flits about on a summer night?

Thirteen

Why should oceans and seas be salty when most rivers and lakes are not? Here is a Taiwanese tale of how the seas became salty.

How Saltwater Came to Fill the Seas

Two hundred years ago, there lived by the banks of a river in Taiwan a ferry operator named Lin Fuhai. Every day he sat waiting for people to approach him at shore's edge, where he would offer to take them across to the other side. In this way, he collected small fees that enabled him to make a living. But Lin Fuhai would never mention the fees at the beginning of the trip, nor would he be angry if none were offered. Whatever his passengers gave him, he accepted gratefully. For small fees, large fees, or no fees at all, Lin Fuhai provided his service cheerfully and sent his passengers away happier than they had been before crossing the river on his ferry.

One day Lin Fuhai was sitting on his boat just peacefully waiting for a customer when along came a Daoist monk dressed in old tattered robes. The monk carried a bundle slung over his back. Suddenly the monk jumped into the boat and said to the ferry operator, "Quickly! Hurry and take me to the other side! I have important business across the way!"

Lin Fuhai immediately rowed the boat to the other side of the river, but as he drew near the shore the monk said, "Oh, my goodness, I was in such a hurry that I forgot something I really need. Please take me back over there quickly!"

Lin Fuhai nodded his head and took the monk back over, but then as soon as they drew near this bank, the monk said in similar manner, "Oh, just forget it . . . I don't need what I forgot so badly after all. Just get me back across, will you?"

And yet again, without a word of complaint, Lin Fuhai rowed the monk back across the lake, only to hear the monk utter the familiar lines as they approached the shore, "I don't want to go here today after all. I've got to return to the original shore." In this manner, Lin Fuhai made the trip back and forth across the lake several times. And, what was remarkable, he obliged the monk without complaint, showing not the slightest displeasure, not one hint of irritation. In the end, the boat came to rest at the original point at shore's edge where the Daoist monk had first boarded the ferry. As he stepped off the boat and made ready to go on his way, the monk offered no money for the ferry operator's labor. Neither did he even have the courtesy to say a word of thanks. Failing to offer so much as a nod good-bye, the monk simply walked away.

But then some five minutes later, the monk came strolling up again, laughed, and said, "I surely caused you a lot of trouble today. To find such a goodhearted and reliable person as yourself in this day and age is not at all easy. I have nothing of value to give you, but I do have this little stone for grinding grain. Please take this as my inadequate little remembrance of your kindness."

"Honorable Dao Master, you are so very thoughtful, but rowing people across to where they need to go is my duty. How can I look upon such activity as trouble?"

"Oh, I know that you are a most sincere man. All you have to do to make this stone work for your good is to utter the magic words, 'Grinding stone, grinding stone, 1-2-3-4-5,' and the stone will turn around and around, bringing you anything that you desire. Whatever you want, the stone will bring to you in the blink of an eye. When you have received all that you want on each occasion, simply say, 'Grinding stone, grinding stone, east-west-left-right,' and the stone will cease bringing things to you."

That evening when Lin Fuhai returned home, he sat in the dim lantern light of his simple hut and repeated the words the Daoist master had taught him: "Grinding stone, grinding stone, 1-2-3-4-5." Sure enough, the little stone came rolling forth. Lin Fuhai said to the stone, "Please bring rice to fill this hungry stomach!" And just as the monk had promised, Lin Fuhai's wish was fulfilled. Grains of the best grade of rice spilled forth unceasingly until he said, "Grinding stone, grinding stone, east-west-left-right." Then the rice immediately stopped flowing.

In this way, Lin Fuhai became a well-fed and wealthy man. But he never forgot his humble origins, and he used his wealth to relieve the suffering of the poor. For many years, he continued to ferry people across the river as always. Then as the years passed and the weariness of old age crept into his bones, Lin Fuhai hired a man to provide ferry service. Lin paid this man, whose name was Wang, very well, and to the customers on his ferry he now offered transport across the river free of charge.

Now as it happened, this man Wang was one of those who is never satisfied with the number of his possessions or the extent of his wealth. Seeing that the humble helmsman had become a wealthy gentleman, Wang couldn't help wanting to know how he had accomplished this. One evening Wang stole into Lin Fuhai's house and happened to catch him with the grinding stone, saying the magic words first taught by the Daoist master. Wang memorized these words, both those that brought forth wished-for items, and those that stopped the flow of such items.

The next day, this Wang fellow heard that Lin Fuhai was going to be taking rice out to people suffering under conditions of a great famine. Wang watched until Lin Fuhai had left, then he seized the grinding stone. He put it on the boat and went with the current downstream. Wang planned to escape with the stone to a place far, far away where he could not be caught. He was sure that he had found a way to live a life of great wealth and ease.

As he drifted downstream, Wang thought, "Now, for what shall I wish? Hmmm . . . I know! Prices for salt are now very high. If I get a large amount of salt, I can make enough money to last me many months, even years. But I won't stop there, of course. For no amount of money is ever enough. I'll keep selling salt for months and months, and on and on, for years to come. I will eventually be the richest man in all Taiwan!"

Wang proceeded to test the magic words: "Grinding stone, grinding stone, 1-2-3-4-5." Just as he hoped, the grinding stone came rolling forth. And just as Wang had seen Lin Fuhai do, he waited for the stone to turn over and over, then he commanded, "Bring me a big bunch of salt!" Precious crystals of salt came pouring into the boat as if out of thin air. On and on the salt poured into the boat. Lin Fuhai sat watching all of this with a greedy grin. But the grin faded as he realized that the boat was beginning to sink. Too much of a good thing! So much salt filled the boat that it was sinking under the heavy load!

Desperately, Lin Fuhai tried to remember the words that would make the salt stop flowing. But in his panic, the words would not come. Laden with its heavy burden of salt, the boat continued to sink, deeper and deeper. Wang drowned as the boat sank all the way to the bottom of the lake under the load of salt that his command had brought forth.

To this day, the grinding stone lies at the bottom of the lake. This lake is connected by a river channel to the sea at the shores of northern Taiwan. As the stone continues to turn in the water, salt continues to flow out of the lake, into the river channel, and on out to sea. And that is how the oceans of the world came to be filled with salt.

Questions for Discussion

1. Have you ever known anyone as patient as Lin Fuhai was with the Daoist monk? If so, who? Does patience always pay off?

2. Lin Fuhai seemed to take the duties of his job seriously. Do you think that most people have this kind of attitude toward their work? Should they?

3. Do you think that Lin Fuhai was still a happy person even after the man that he hired stole his magical grinding stone? Explain.

Suggestions for Class Activities

1. Take turns telling made-up tales of how saltwater came to fill the seas. Have students then draw detailed illustrations based on their favorite stories.

2. Conduct a class research project on the importance of salt. Individual or group projects could be divided so as to explore such themes as the evolutionary origin of salt in the seas, the importance of salt in human economic activities, how salt has been controlled by the rulers of countries, and the various ways that salt has been extracted for commercial use. An excellent resource for the teacher would be Mark Kurlansky's Salt: A World History (New York: Walker and Company, 2002).

Fourteen

Have you ever thought about how thunder and lightning originated? Here is a story that gives a mythological explanation for the origin of lightning.

The God of Thunder and the Mother of Lightning

One day the Heavenly Emperor looked down from Heaven on high to earth below. He said to himself, "It is about time that I conduct a good investigation of conditions among the people of earth." Upon investigation, though, the Heavenly Emperor trembled in anger at what he saw. In too many places, people were not treating other people as they should. At one out-of-the-way spot, for example, the Heavenly Emperor could see a pack of robbers stealing the goods of a traveling salesman. To make matters worse, the robbers pushed the poor fellow over a precipice to erase all traces of their evil deed. They were sure that passersby would now have no chance of discovering their act and reporting it to local authorities.

Now how could the great, benevolent Heavenly Emperor allow such a flagrant violation of proper conduct? Such a terrible deed was an affront to Heaven itself. He immediately issued an order to his assistant, Lei Gong, the God of Thunder, to use his powers to end the lives of these two robbers who were disturbing the public order.

In the moment when Lei Gong made good the death warrant, all was dark and hazy upon the earth. Then, from the sky came an awe-inspiring crash of thunder. Lei Gong was striking with his great iron spear. From the tip of his spear shot an electrical current that sent all the robbers on earth to their deaths. Not a single person now stirred upon the firmament who desired to rob others of their property. In this manner, Lei Gong fulfilled the command of the Heavenly Emperor to judge the good and evil in the hearts of humankind. Wherever Lei Gong found those who might do harm to fellow human beings, he eliminated them, and so he continued until every last person of such inclination was removed from the face of the earth.

One rainy day Lei Gong as usual patrolled the earth into all of those areas where the moisture that he brought forth penetrated. He wielded the familiar iron spear in his dancing hands, roaming everywhere he suspected the lurking of an evil heart. He came at one point to the entrance of a rural village, where he spied a woman just as she took a whole bowl of what Lei Gong assumed was rice and dumped it in a ditch. Lei Gong felt that a person who valued the precious grains of rice so little was truly reprehensible. Accordingly, Lei Gong gave the woman a mighty jolt with his iron spear.

But gods, like human beings, are sometimes too hasty. Lei Gong should have investigated before sending forth the jolt from his spear. The woman Lei Gong had believed to be a despicable creature lived in a household with her husband and his elderly mother. They were very poor. The filial daughter-in-law frequently gave this elderly one a bit of gruel made from boiling rice. For herself she saved the husk of the rice to boil for a soup. This humble soup was the younger woman's main food. After eating the soup, she would take the dregs formed by the rice husks and dump them in a ditch. So, in fact, what Lei Gong had seen her toss out wasn't the precious grains of rice but rather the coarse outer covering of the grain.

The Heavenly Emperor came to know that Lei Gong had struck a most filial daughter-in-law. Taking vigorous action to right the wrong that had been done, the mighty god raised the woman up into Heaven with one sweep of his mighty hand. The Heavenly Emperor installed the filial woman in his pantheon. He invested her with powers that brought her the title of Lei Mu, Mother of Lightning. She became the wife of Lei Gong, the very god who had wronged her with his rash action.

Husband and wife lived very happily together as they coordinated their work for the Heavenly Emperor. From the day of their marriage forward, Lei Mu's gift of lightning prevented Lei Gong from the errors that darkness can bring. Now, before he sent his thunder crashing to the earth below, Lei Gong asked his wife to issue a flash of light so that he could properly inspect every little thing. Guided by the brilliant light provided by Lei Mu, Lei Gong could now avoid the kind of error that once had inflicted her with such an unjust blow.

Questions for Discussion

1. At one point in this story, the God of Thunder jumps to the wrong conclusion about the young woman sifting the grain. Do you think that people often don't think carefully enough before they act? Give examples of such behavior.

2. Why does the story indicate that one can always see lightning from Lei Mu before hearing the thunder produced by Lei Gong?

3. What do you learn about the Taiwanese ideal of the good daughter-in-law from this tale?

Suggestions for Class Activities

1. Read selections from Norse, Greek, and Roman mythology that deal with the gods of thunder and lightning. Discuss with the class the similarities and differences in these myths.

2. Have the students individually write their own mythological tales about the origin of thunder and lightning. After finishing rough and polished drafts, have them read their stories aloud to each other in class.

3. Have students research thunder and lightning. What causes thunder? What causes lightning? Are there some places that have more thunder and lightning than others? What are some of the bad things that have happened as a result of thunder and lightning? Do thunder and lightning have any positive effects?

Fifteen

People throughout history have associated certain plants with particular magical or healing powers. This story tells you about a plant that gives new meaning to the term, "sea change."

The Strange Plant Known as White-Horse Mateng

Three hundred years ago, the eastern part of Beimen District in Tainan County lay entirely on a seashore. A small island, also called Beimen by the people of the area, lay very close to that shore. In time, the buildup of silt and sediment in the space between Beimen Island and the shore caused the island to disappear.

It is said that the Beimen Island of old had a mountain by the name of Stone Wells' Foot, on which grew an exceedingly rare plant. The plant was pure white from root to leaf. The island's inhabitants called the plant White-Horse Mateng.

One day a British ship sailed near Beimen Island. Through their binoculars the sailors aboard could see a tree rising in an umbrella shape atop the island. It shown so brightly that it seemed to emit a glowing white light from the interior of the forest that lay near the island's shore. The captain of the ship, fascinated and curious, sent some of his mates forth to investigate. They discovered that the glow came from the tree's reflection of the sun's rays. What a wondrous plant to reflect so strongly the natural light of the sun! The mates dug up the tree and took it back with them to their ship.

Strangely enough, when the White-Horse Mateng was lowered into the water, the salty ocean became a freshwater lake. The British stayed in the area for several days, keeping the White-Horse Mateng plant all the while. The magical plant enabled them to overcome the problem that always challenges those who set to sea of carrying sufficient fresh water. These British sailors had no trouble maintaining a constant supply.

But something unexpected happened. After a few days, the mountain of Stone Well's Foot suddenly emitted a thunderous roar. The peak of the mountain cracked open and soon filled the gap between mountain and shore. The British ship carrying the White-Horse Mateng exploded and sank to the bottom of the sea. The White-Horse Mateng drifted into the sea as the ship sank. From that day forward, the plant's magical nature gave the waters along this coastal area of Taiwan a distinctive feature: the water remained saltless, providing clear and tasty fresh water for all Taiwanese fishers and others working and living along that part of the coast.

Questions for Discussion

1. Is your town close to a lake, river, or ocean? Often bodies of water and other places in nature are the source of tales and legends. Share any tales you know that are associated with places of nature in your community, especially those connected to bodies of water.

2. The "White-Horse Mateng" plant of this story had the power to turn the sea into a saltless body of water. What advantages does fresh water have over salty water? Would people living along the shore feel differently from sailors about the advantages of fresh, versus salty, water? Explain.

3. The places in this tale have interesting names, such as White-Horse Mateng and Stone Well's Foot. Share opinions as to the most interesting place names within fifty or so miles of your town or city.

Suggestions for Class Activities

1. This story selection is full of picturesque scenes: the glow of White-Horse Mateng, sea adventurers discovering the sea turned into freshwater, the eruption of Stone Well's Foot, and the filling in of the sea. Have each student draw or paint her or his favorite scene from the story, taking care to present the scene in detail, either as described in the story or from the student's imagination.

2. Discuss with your class the use of the sea as the setting for works of quality literature. Use this as an opportunity to introduce students to the work of Robert Louis Stevenson, reading all or sections of either *Treasure Island* or *Kidnapped.* Have each student write a story based on one of her or his experiences with water.

3. Is it possible that there really is such a plant as White-Horse Mateng with properties that allow it to remove salt from the water? Research and write a report on your findings.

Part Four

Taiwanese Sayings and Their Origins

Sixteen

Have you ever thought about the origin of expressions such as "Three in the hand are worth two in the bush," or "Absence makes the heart grow fonder"? Here is a tale about the origin of a common Taiwanese expression.

When Three People Have Only Five Eyes

Among the Taiwanese people, there is a well-known saying that goes, "If three people have only five eyes, long and short legs may not be mentioned." What on earth could such a strange saying mean? Its origin may be found in the following story.

In the old days, there was a most proficient matchmaker who sought to bring together a young, one-eyed woman with a young man who walked with a limp because his legs were different lengths. Before introducing them, she said not a word about the one's physical deficiency to the other. And so she told the lame young man that when he was introduced to the young woman, he should place his shortened leg on the threshold of the door so as to affect an evenly matched pair. In similar fashion, the matchmaker told the young woman that she should sit behind the decorative screen in the room and show only her good side. The matchmaker further instructed the young woman to cast a pleasing and shy look at the young man, as if from two good eyes.

The plan succeeded, or at least the young people came away from the meeting exceedingly pleased with one another. They readily agreed to the prospective marriage. So as to head off any discord that might come when the young couple discovered the previously concealed flaws, the matchmaker spoke the following words in private counsel with each party: "If three people have only five eyes, long and short legs may not be mentioned." Each of the two young people thought that these words were rather strange. But the speaker was the matchmaker who had brought them together, and everything else she had told them seemed to make sense. So they let her strange words go. Neither young person suspected anything when she added, "Since the matter of matrimony is something about which the two of you have agreed, you may not renege on this matter of your own consent." Neither the young woman nor the young man had seen anything about the other that made either want to renege on their engagement.

But in fact, each of the young people did in time come to express dissatisfaction. Each reprimanded the matchmaker for concealing the full truth about the other. But the matchmaker replied in a self-righteous and indignant manner, "Did I not say that if three people have only five eyes, long and short legs may not be mentioned? Could you not think just a bit more deeply? Obviously, one of us must have had only one good eye, and one of us must have had one leg shorter than the other." Then she added, "You may not now go back on your marital agreement, for as I told you, because this matter of matrimony is something about which the two of you have agreed, you may not renege on this matter of your own consent."

The story goes that in time the young woman and man were glad that they had made the agreement. They honored the words of the matchmaker and remained husband and wife. They raised three children together and lived long lives of great happiness together, overcoming their previous biases about the particular physical challenge that each faced.

This story and the saying derived from it, though, do contain a message of caution. In time, the saying came to mean that whenever the ground rules for a situation are known ahead of time, the parties involved should accept all resulting circumstances without complaint.

Questions for Class Discussion

1. The matchmaker, or "go-between," occupied an important role in traditional Taiwanese society. Can you think of any societies that have or did have matchmakers?

2. How have husbands and wives usually been chosen in the United States? Does anyone other than the young people themselves play a role?

Suggestions for Class Activities

1. Read selections from the E. D. Hirsch Core Knowledge books that give examples of common expressions. Have the students discuss where they think such expressions might have originated. Alternatively, students might write stories about the origins of expressions. (E. D. Hirsch, Jr., ed., *What Your [Kindergartner–Sixth Grader] Needs to Know.* New York: Doubleday, 1991–1996. The first volume in this series, *What Your First Grader Needs to Know,* was published in 1991. The fifth- and sixth-grade volumes appeared in 1993, and then the editor went back and added a volume for kindergartners in 1996.)

2. Have the students each compose three expressions that teach a moral or offer advice. After they have individually composed their expressions, hold a class discussion in which the students share their expressions and decide which of these they would really like to see catch on as common saying used by generations to come.

Seventeen

Have you ever known anyone who liked to pretend that she or he knew more than the person really did, or had abilities that she or he did not really possess? Here is story about one such person, and the fate that he met because of his pretense.

The Tiger-Nosed Lion Who Wanted to Burn Up Heaven

On Taiwan a person with a particularly keen sense of smell is called a "Tiger-Nosed Lion." The association comes from similar pronunciations of two sets of characters for the Mandarin language, one meaning "lion with the nose of a tiger," and the other meaning "good nose."

The link between the two expressions has been further strengthened by a story about a man by the name of Hu Bishi. The characters of this man's name are the same as those for "Tiger-Nosed Lion." In the story, Hu Bishi convinces people that he has a particularly keen sense of smell.

Hu Bishi was one of those husbands who had no regular source of income. His wife provided virtually all of their living. She had brought a nice dowry into their union, and she made some additional money through her sewing and craft skills and by raising chickens. Hu Bishi's wife was one of the most truly patient and loving people on earth. She was forever hearing about and forgiving the wild schemes of her husband that inevitably ended in financial failure.

One day, for example, Hu Bishi saw a flock of white egrets as he was strolling by a rice paddy. He thought to himself, "If I were to raise a flock of egrets, I certainly could make a good bit of money." He then proceeded to make an offer of purchase to the farmer working in the rice paddy. The farmer could hardly believe that such a foolish character had come his way. The farmer gleefully collected

N.T.* $300 from Hu Bishi, and then he added insult to injury by telling the scheming ne'er-do-well: "When you want the egrets to follow you, all you have to do is yell, 'It's finished! It's finished!' The egrets will then obediently line up behind you and follow you home."

The farmer chuckled to himself as he strolled away. Wishing to return home, Hu Bishi tried out the farmer's advice. He called out to his newly purchased egrets, "It's finished! It's finished!" But all the white egrets flew away. Hu Bishi was very angry, but what could he do? By the time he had calmed down a bit and his head had begun to clear, the farmer who had pulled the trick was nowhere in sight. Hu Bishi turned and headed for home, dreading that he would have to tell his wife he had once again squandered her money.

As he walked along, Hu Bishi thought of his many recent failed schemes. He thought again of being tricked into paying so much money for egrets, birds that roam wild and are free to those who can get them. He grew angry again—more and more so as time went on. He was so beside himself that he did not see a big pile of pig manure at roadside. Two mama pigs came along in front of him and at first prevented Hu Bishi from falling into the manure. But Hu wasn't paying attention and bumped into the pigs; his momentum pushed them forward, and together they fell into the pile of manure. Hu Bishi was now so mad that he couldn't see straight. But if his eyes were not doing him much good, and his nose had to deal with something far from good, his ears soon began to treat him better. In time he overheard a flurry of conversation about the search for a couple of pigs. Quickly he thought up yet another money-making stratagem. Full of such thoughts, he scurried back home.

Upon returning home, Hu Bishi said to his wife, "I must confess that I once again frittered away all of the money that you gave me. But just now I thought up an ingenious plan. You know what a keen sense of smell I have. I have decided that I am going to make us a lot of money with this skill of mine. When people find that they are missing something dear to them, I will hire myself out to them. I will sniff my way to whatever it is that they have lost." So very proud of this plan, Hu Bishi wore a self-satisfied grin as he waited for his wife's response.

And his wife was surely one of the most patient people on earth. She seemed to have never-ending faith that her husband would one day succeed. "Really?" she responded. Sniff your way to success, huh? Well, consider this for your first job: I just happened to hear that the Ah Laishu family has lost sight of a couple of their mama pigs. I suppose there's no harm in your going out to see if you can find them."

*N.T. stands for New Taiwan, or the New Taiwan dollar, the currency used in Taiwan since 1949.

Hu Bishi went out and offered his services to the Ah Laishu family. They thought his claims for the power of his nose were rather goofy, but they told him to go ahead and try to find their pigs. Hu Bishi then went through quite a charade, pretending that he was in earnest search for the pigs. Only slowly did he make his way to the big pile of manure. There, still close by, he found the pigs. From that day forward, Hu Bishi's reputation as an ingenious finder of lost things spread far and wide across the island of Taiwan.

But Hu Bishi was unsettled of spirit. He lived in fear that someone would discover he was a fake. So Hu Bishi turned his attention to a plan for strengthening his claims to have a magically keen sense of smell. One night while Zhang Dacai, the village leader, was sleeping, Hu Bishi snuck into his house and stole his finest robe. Then he took the robe and hid it in a big haystack lying in a field.

Sure enough, the next day Zhang Dacai discovered that someone had taken his robe. Thinking of what people had said about Hu Bishi's magical nostrils, the village leader sent an attendant to request the services of Mr. Hu. Hu Bishi of course accepted the job. Pretending that he was extending great effort and persevering under extreme hardship, he first sniffed out virtually the whole field. He came at last to the haystack. Letting everyone see that he felt that he was getting close, he moved nearer to the haystack, sniffing furiously. Then he yelled out in great excitement, "I found it! I found it! Who would have thought that someone would have put it in such a place?"

Zhang Dacai was overjoyed at the recovery of his expensive robe. The village leader gave a big feast in Hu Bishi's honor. With heartfelt gratitude, Zhang toasted Hu with many compliments. At the end of the party, he rewarded the man of the supposedly great nose with 1,200 silver pieces.

Not long after that celebration, Hu Bishi's reputation spread across the Taiwan Strait, throughout mainland China, and eventually to the court of the emperor. At about the same time that news of the great-nosed one arrived at the imperial court, the emperor's jade chop [a stamp that imprints one's name on official documents] turned up missing. The ruler of all China was heartbroken over the loss. Thinking of Hu Bishi's reputation as a finder of lost objects, the emperor dispatched a messenger to secure the services of this supposedly remarkable man.

With this turn of circumstances, Hu Bishi was most shaken, indeed. How in the world was he going to find the emperor's chop? And yet soon the emperor's sedan chair arrived to carry him to the palace. Hu had no choice but to stick out his chest, hold his head high, and seat himself in the sedan chair.

Once in the sedan chair, though, Hu Bishi's fears rose anew: What strategy could he use to find the imperial chop? Along the road, Hu Bishi absentmindedly took note of a bunch of mud snails and some leeches, all in a hassle over something. More out of a rattled mental state than any real disgust with the sight of the crawling things, the nose wizard mumbled, "Snails—leeches—you should just die!"

Now it just so happened that one of the men carrying the sedan chair was named Tian Lo, which means "snail," and the other was named Mao Zhi, which means "leech." These two ne'er-do-wells had managed to get jobs in the imperial house, but they didn't recognize a good thing when they had it. They had been talked into stealing the imperial chop by a dishonest court official. Now, hearing Hu Bishi say that the snail and the leech should die, Tian Lo and Mao Zhi fell to their knees and begged, "Sir! Kind sir! Please spare our lives, and we will tell you where we have hidden the emperor's chop!"

And so it came to pass that the two thieves led Hu Bishi straight to an old well in the capital. Luck paid another visit to Mr. Keen Nose. The emperor was, of course, exceedingly pleased and sought to reward Hu Bishi magnificently for his efforts. But Hu Bishi had a request that he thought better than money. He said, "My emperor, I'd like to go to Heaven to look around for a spell. You are the Son of Heaven. Could you arrange for a ladder to be lowered to earth so that I might have this wish?"

The emperor, considered by the Chinese to have inherited his position with the approval of Heaven, thought for a while. The Son of Heaven did not act upon such requests often. But so thankful was he to Hu Bishi for finding his chop that he decided to make the request in the nose detective's honor. Soon a ladder stretching to Heaven came falling toward earth. But as he ascended the ladder, Hu Bishi found that a few rungs on the ladder were missing. He cast his eyes toward earth and, as if calling to the emperor, said, "Please, quickly help me *shao tian*."

Now the term *shao tian* is an expression used by the Taiwanese that means "to overcome difficulty." Not all of the gods were familiar with the expression. Lei Gong, the God of Thunder, upon hearing Hu Bishi's request, thought that a man was asking that Heaven be burned and rose up in great anger. He lifted Hu Bishi high into the sky and gave him a roller-coaster view of Heaven before casting him heavily toward the earth. The hapless Hu Bishi lay in a heap of broken bones. His schemes had finally caught up with him. There would be no more claims for the magic of his nose.

The story goes, though, that the fall of Hu Bishi gave life to another creature. The bones of Hu Bishi eventually metamorphosed into many tiny ants, and from this incident, ants joined the other small and large creatures of the earth.

Questions for Discussion

1. Why do you think that Hu Bishi's wife trusted him with the N.T. $300 when she surely must have known that he had squandered money many times before? Would you have trusted Hu Bishi with the money?

2. Why do you think that people so readily believed that Hu Bishi had the power to find lost items through the power of his nose? Do people often believe the claims of others without checking to make sure that they are true?

3. What does this story ultimately seem to say about the Taiwanese opinion of such a pretender? Do the Taiwanese seem to disapprove or approve of the behavior of someone like Hu Bishi?

Suggestions for Class Activities

1. Have the students compose a story as a whole class, with each student contributing a line in succession. Have the first person (ideally a student, but the teacher may go first if students have a hard time thinking of the first line) start with one line only, then the second person contributes another, then the third person, and so on until the story has reached satisfactory completion. Have the story focus on a character similar to Hu Bishi, someone who likes to pretend that she or he has abilities that the person does not possess.

2. Record the students' composition of their story as they are creating the tale orally. Type the story for them, and then have each student do one illustration of some scene from the tale. Put the story and the illustrations into book form and share the story with other classes.

3. What kind of currency is actually used in Taiwan today? Conduct research in the library or on the Internet to find out what N.T. $300 translates into in U.S. money. Have students design their own currency, drawing illustrations of various bills and coins with images of important people and places on each.

Eighteen

Have you ever heard the story "The Boy Who Cried Wolf"? Here is a version told by the Taiwanese.

Reckless Words Spoken Once Too Often

There was in former days a boy named Chi-Ah whose very character seemed to force lies from his mouth. His days were full of falsehoods spoken for the fun of fooling his fellow villagers. Accordingly, the boy was known as Baizei Chi-Ah. *Baizei,* literally "White Thief," means one who engages in wild and reckless talk.

One day Chi-Ah went to the local market. Seeing that the business of the peddlers was lagging, Chi-Ah popped out with, "Are the vegetables you're selling quite fresh? Today my uncle is celebrating his birthday, so this evening he'll be giving a feast of one hundred tables. He sent me to market to buy the food for the feast."

Now the meat sellers and the vegetable sellers heard this news with great interest and their lagging spirits began to rise. They surrounded Chi-Ah gleefully, playing up to him, each peddler flooding him with courteous and flattering words:

"Chi-Ah, my brother, have a cool fruit drink! You must surely want to buy a big batch of vegetables!"

"Brother Chi-Ah, let me pour your fruit drink for you. My price is the fairest around!" Such words came from all directions. Chi-Ah became, for the moment, the sole focus of the peddlers' attentions.

Chi-Ah walked back to his uncle's house, saw that his uncle wasn't home, then said to his uncle's wife, "Oh, Auntie, it's terrible! Uncle has fallen into a lake! He's drowned, Auntie!" So saying, Chi-Ah ran away as fast as smoke swept up in a strong wind.

Chi-Ah's aunt followed fast behind, barely able to see as her eyes filled with tears and her face became a salty lake. Chi-Ah was too fast for her. He ran to a nearby village where his uncle often spent time with friends. Sure enough, he found his uncle chatting in the home of a friend. "Uncle!" exclaimed Chi-Ah. "Your house has burned to the ground. I'm afraid that Auntie was trapped in the room where she had been sitting!"

Chi-Ah's uncle immediately scurried away in the direction of home, but on his way he discovered his wife running all in huff, eyes filled with tears. Husband and wife soon came to understand that Chi-Ah had played one of his tricks on them. And for this trick, Chi-Ah paid with an evening spent in the woodshed, to which his uncle sent him as punishment. As dawn came next morning to the lovely island of Taiwan, Chi-Ah's uncle opened the woodshed, saw a soundly sleeping Chi-Ah, and asked with wonder, "Last night was so chilly. How did you manage to sleep with so few clothes and no blanket to keep you warm?" (Although Taiwan generally has quite warm weather, winter nights and some days can feel cold to the Taiwanese.)

Chi-Ah replied, "Though I do not appear to have much on, I did put on my warmest undershirt. It really did the trick! I wasn't cold in the least!"

This made sense to Chi-Ah's uncle. Wanting such a warm undershirt for himself, he offered Chi-Ah ten silver pieces for it. Tattered and torn though the undershirt was, it had apparently kept Chi-Ah warm all through the chilly night.

Next day Chi-Ah's uncle wore the undershirt as he took a long walk in the countryside. He found, though, that he still trembled in the face of a stiff cold wind. Realizing that Chi-Ah had tricked him again, he rushed home once more to see that his nephew paid for the trouble that he had caused. And he wanted to make sure that Chi-Ah paid back the money he had charged for the useless long undershirt.

Returning to the village full of anger, Chi-Ah's uncle found the naughty boy sitting in the front court of their home. Intent on punishing him, uncle's attitude softened when Chi-Ah seemed to be truly sorry that the undershirt had not kept his uncle warm. Chi-Ah had already spent the money, but the boy expressed firm willingness to return the ten silver pieces and then some. Chi-Ah said that he had a plan and would return with the money later that afternoon. With that, Chi-Ah grabbed a blanket and left the house. Chi-Ah's uncle decided to give the boy a chance to come up with the money.

As he walked along the road, Chi-Ah wondered, "Now, how can I come up with those ten silver pieces?" It just so happened that at about that time, he ran across a hunchbacked old man tending a flock of ducks en route to the local market. Chi-Ah once again cast an impudent eye upon another opportunity to make mischief. He told the old man that if he would just put his ducks in the blanket, he could cure himself of his hunched back. But of course after the ducks crawled up into the blanket, Chi-Ah quickly tied them up and headed to market himself. The sale of these, he hoped, would bring him enough to repay his uncle. And the sale did indeed bring him well over the ten silver pieces that he needed to pay his uncle back.

Chi-Ah made quite a fuss as he returned to his uncle's house, saying, "Oh, uncle, I can pay you back and then some! I've become wealthy! The Sea Dragon King wants me for a son-in-law and has bestowed many pieces of silver on me as a gift! So here are the ten silver pieces that I owe you. And, here, take three more!"

Chi-Ah's uncle was astonished. He said in a tone that showed his sense of wonder, "Oh, Chi-Ah! Have you really seen the palace of the Sea Dragon King? Isn't it a glittering sight to see? Oh, do take me to meet this father-in-law of yours!"

Now, Chi-Ah of course had never even met the Sea Dragon King, but he decided to take his lie a little further. Chi-Ah said his uncle, "What a great idea, uncle! Let's take a rowboat out to sea where my friends from the palace of the Sea Dragon King will see us and escort us to that grand dwelling!"

So Chi-Ah and his uncle set off for the seashore. Once there, they got in a rowboat and rowed out far away from shore. When they arrived at the middle of the ocean, uncle spied a hole in the boat's bottom and saw that they had already started to sink. Yet Chi-Ah seemed frozen in fear. He offered no help. And because he had really never encountered the Sea Dragon King or any of his assistants before, Chi-Ah could not have expected what happened next.

The Sea Dragon King knew of Chi-Ah's lies, and he was particularly mad that the young man had involved his name in one of them. Accordingly, he had sent several of his patrol officers to meet Chi-Ah and bring him before his court. Fortunately, these patrol officers arrived just in time to save Chi-Ah and his uncle from sinking. Having completed the rescue, the officers returned to tell of the incident to the Sea Dragon King. Upon hearing their report, the king was deeply angered. He resolved to discipline severely this "White Thief Chi-Ah," who so loved to cause misery with his lies.

The Sea Dragon King sent three patrol officers to hide in the depths of the ocean to look for Chi-Ah making his return to shore. In time, Chi-Ah came in sight, rowing his boat toward shore. But he sensed that something was up and quickly came up with a plan. He said to the sea patrol officers: "Oh! Oh! Your arrival is so very timely! The great Jade Emperor has requested that I cut up some driftwood. That net of yours will be perfect for gathering up the wood. The Jade Emperor will be so pleased. You are sure to reap a great reward!"

Now, of course, the net the three patrol officers carried had been intended to ensnare Chi-Ah. They didn't know what to make of his words. In the end, they decided to give the net to him. They then returned to the palace of the Sea Dragon King to make their report.

The Sea Dragon King was thoroughly disgusted that his officers had been so easily fooled. This time, he sent forth his greatest general to shore, riding a stout, swift stallion. The general had strictest orders to capture Chi-Ah and bring him to trial at the court of the Sea Dragon King. By the time the general came ashore, Chi-Ah had already landed safely on the beach. He had managed to talk a farmer out of his ox and was riding along on the beast's back. In time, the general dispatched by the Sea Dragon King caught up with Chi-Ah. Not knowing who he was, he said to him, "Please, young lad, do tell me if you know a boy about your age in these parts who loves to tell lies? His name is Chi-Ah."

"Oh, yes . . . that guy!" replied Chi-Ah. "He lives far away, clear on the other side of the island. You'll take a long time trying to capture him riding that horse."

"Oh, no," replied the general. "If this Chi-Ah is anywhere on the island of Taiwan, I'll catch him. This horse of mine is a One Thousand-Mile Stallion. It is so named because it is able to travel swiftly at least one thousand miles in the course of a single day."

Chi-Ah did not miss a beat. "But how can a One Thousand-Mile Stallion be faster than this Ten Thousand-Mile Ox?" he asked the general. "That's what I'm riding. It can travel ten thousand miles in a single day. I can see that you, mighty general, must be traveling on a very special mission. So I'll exchange my 'Ten Thousand-Mile Ox' for your 'Thousand-Mile Stallion.' "

Having so tricked the Sea Dragon King's general, Chi-Ah rode his new stallion home. Very weary after so many adventures, Chi-Ah lay down to take a long nap. After a while, Chi-Ah was startled from his nap by the frantic cry of his uncle's cat. The house was hotter than the hottest summer day on tropical southern Taiwan. Rubbing the sleep from his eyes, he saw the cat, looking as scared as the mouse that it held in its teeth by the tail. The house was engulfed in flames. A kerosene lantern lay overturned on the floor. Chi-Ah quickly saw what must have happened: in chasing the mouse, the cat had overturned the lantern. The lantern had caused a great fire—a real fire this time, not the false fire that he had reported to his uncle, not the fire of his imagination that he had falsely reported had taken his aunt's life.

Chi-Ah cried out in desperation. He was pulling no trick this time. These flames were real, and they would take his life if he did not get out of the house soon. He cried out, "Help! Save me! The inside of the house is on fire! I'm trapped. Oh, somebody, please help me!"

Chi-Ah's uncle and aunt were out working in their fields. They could hear the voice crying out to them. It was faint, but they could hear the cries for help clearly enough. Other villagers were close enough to hear the cries even more clearly, but none were in a position to see the house. The smoke had not become visible nor did it produce enough of a smell to serve as clear warning that a fire had indeed broken out. Uncle, aunt, and the other villagers did recognize that the voice crying out to them was that of Chi-Ah. And they thought that the boy must surely be up to another one of his pranks.. . .

Questions for Discussion

1. Are there similarities between this tale and "The Boy Who Cried Wolf"? Are there differences?

2. Is there such a thing as a "good" prank? If so, what are some examples of good and bad pranks?

3. What does it mean when people say that someone "cried 'wolf' once too often"?

Suggestions for Class Activities

1. As told in this tale, Chi-Ah deals with the representatives of the Sea Dragon King, but he never sees the Sea Dragon King, nor does he ever make it to the king's palace. Have students draw or paint the Sea Dragon King in his palace, then have them share their creations to compare how each person imagined them to look. Are there any similarities? Important differences?

2. Have the students think about what would have happened had the three patrol officers in the story captured Chi-Ah and brought him before the Sea Dragon King. Because the theme of the tale demands that Chi-Ah be free at the end of the story to meet the consequences of his trickery, it would be logical to have Chi-Ah eventually escaping from the palace. As an exercise in creative writing, have each student write a story that tells what would have happened to Chi-Ah at the court of the Sea Dragon King, and how he would have escaped. Once completed, allow time for each student to share her or his ideas by reading the story aloud in class.

Color Plates

Children feeding ducklings at a pond on the campus of National Chenggong University, Taiwan.

Puppets and other goods for sale near Lugang's Tianhou Temple.

Fisher-folk ready squid for sale in Magong, Penghu.

Young and old worshippers and offerers of incense at Taibei's Longshan Temple.

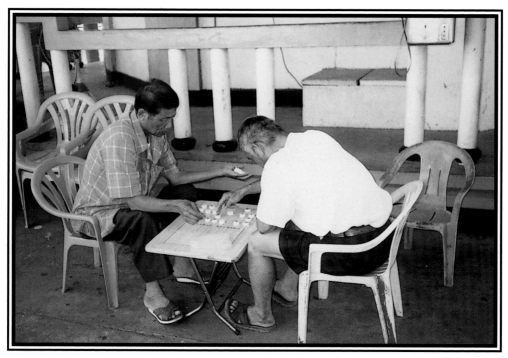

Xiangqi (Chinese chess) players at a temple in Taiwan.

A water buffalo, traditionally the most important draft animal on Taiwanese farms.

Rice paddies remain the most notable features of Taiwan's increasingly diversified agricultural landscape.

A boatman on his craft in the harbor of Magong, Penghu.

Cloud-strewn mountains of central Taiwan's Alishan area.

Statue of Milofo, "The Laughing Buddha," at the mountainside Faxing Zen
Temple of Gaoxiong, Taiwan.

Skillfully carved religious figures produced and sold by one of Lugang's many artisans.

The great red-faced Daoist deity Guangong, God of war and commerce.

Shrine of an important female ancestor in a Taiwanese lineage-extended family group.

A traditional Taiwanese gravesite on Xiaomen Island of the Penghu group,
to the west of Taiwan proper.

Key statue of Koxinga (Zheng Chenggong) at the shrine built in his honor in Tainan, Taiwan.

A sign calling for Taiwanese independence, with an interesting difference of scale between Taiwan and China.

Part Five

Taiwanese Legends and Historical Tales

Nineteen

Do you know some legends about famous figures in United States history, such as the presidents George Washington and Abraham Lincoln? Here are several legends that the Taiwanese tell about the famous historical figure Koxinga, about whom readers may learn in the historical overview at the beginning of the book.

Iron Anvil Mountain and the Well of Koxinga

The mountain known as Iron Anvil Mountain in Da Jia District of Taizhong County is a sight familiar throughout the island. People of the region gave the mountain this name because it is indeed shaped like an iron anvil. A well atop Iron Anvil Mountain is steep and a full kilometer deep. The water is sweet and magnificent to the taste, and the well has never to this day run dry.

A legend passed down through the centuries has it that when Koxinga (Zheng Chenggong) passed Iron Anvil Mountain with his armies, he came into the territory occupied by aborigines. The temperature at the time was scorching hot, and there was an apparent scarcity of water. Many soldiers and horses dropped to their deaths. The story goes that Koxinga pulled out his trusty sword and stuck it into the ground. As if his actions had brought forth the mercy of Heaven, a fountain rose in the air almost immediately upon the thrust of his sword.

After Koxinga's army gained access to the well atop Iron Anvil Mountain, its fighting spirit rose considerably, and the soldiers rushed forth to victory over the Dutch. People in later times dubbed this well Guo Xing Jing, or "Koxinga's Well." They also called it Sword Well, in remembrance of Koxinga's effective thrust of his sword. (Taiwan's people called Zheng Chenggong "Guo Xingye," after the name given to Zheng by an emperor of the Ming dynasty). According to legend, every year at the time of the Dragon Boat Festival when people look down into the depths of the well, one can see the image of the sword. People of this district in Taizhong County firmly believe that the water from Koxinga's Well has the power to cure many diseases.

At one point in Koxinga's struggle against the Dutch, his army was entrapped, and provisions were running low. Legend has it that even his best soldiers had to catch snails and eat them to survive. The story goes that his soldiers discovered that as they finished eating the snails and cast aside the shells, meat began to refill the shells. The army of Koxinga never again had to fear starvation. This is taken as an indication that Koxinga had divine help. Some people in the region claim that they have seen snails of Iron Anvil Mountain regenerate themselves in this way.

Another story from this legend-rich region has it that every year during the Qing Ming Festival countless eagles fly forth from Phoenix Mountain to Guo Xing Jing Well, weeping loudly as they fly. The eagles continue the cries that began with the military losses suffered atop Phoenix Mountain. The belief is that the soldiers' spirits now dwell within the eagles. These eagles fly forth every year, it is said, to pay homage to the spirit and to the memory of Koxinga.

Questions for Discussion

1. What legends do you know about George Washington, Abraham Lincoln, Daniel Boone, Davy Crockett, Annie Oakley, Calamity Jane, and other historical figures in the United States? Share these with the class.

2. Why do you think that people tell stories that are not literally true about historical figures whom they admire?

3. Many times there is some fundamental truth behind a legend, even if the events in the story did not happen as they are presented. What do you think might be the fundamental truth behind each of the legends told in this tale about Koxinga?

Suggestions for Class Activities

1. Use the story of Koxinga as an opportunity to talk about the nature of legends, distinguishing this genre from myths, allegories, and other similar literary forms. Use the E. D. Hirsch Core Knowledge series as resource books for other legends that convey the importance of certain historical figures to various societies. (E. D. Hirsch, Jr., ed., *What Your [Kindergartner–Sixth Grader] Needs to Know.* New York: Doubleday, 1991–1996. The first volume in this series, *What Your First Grader Needs to Know,* was published in 1991. The fifth- and sixth-grade volumes appeared in 1993, and then the editor added a volume for kindergartners in 1996.)

2. Have the students pick their favorite among these three legends about the exploits and special powers of Koxinga and illustrate the chosen legend through an artistic medium of their choice. Offer each student the opportunity to present an artistic rendering of the story through the visual arts of painting, sculpture, or graphic design; a dramatic performance; a musical composition with lyrics; or a poetic version of the story. Have the students share their artistic renderings with the rest of the class.

3. Conduct research in the library or on the Internet to find information about Koxinga and the history surrounding him. What do we know about his family, origins, and rise to power? What elements in this tale are true?

Twenty

Have you ever considered how the location of a house, the direction which a building faces, or the placement of a garden might affect the attitudes and lives of the people who occupy or use these? People in Chinese societies like Taiwan have developed the study of such effects into an art form (some would claim a science). It is called fengshui *(pronounced "feng-shway"). Here is a story about the* fengshui *of a mountain cave, the roads leading to it, and the surrounding community.*

The Luck of Zhishan

It is said that Zhishan, a mountain in the Shilin District of Taibei, once had hordes of bats. Because bats are a symbol of good fortune, people of the area regarded Zhishan as a blessed place. Those people who lived on the mountain itself considered themselves to be the luckiest of all. They happily went about their lives assuming that they would receive extra blessings because of the presence of the good luck bats. It was with extra confidence that they observed traditional customs associated with such important times as the Lunar New Year.

In those days, lanterns were hung all around Zhishan at the time of the Festival of Lights that followed the Lunar New Year. From the first through the fifteenth days of the first month of the New Year, people from all around Zhishan could see the brilliant light of hundreds of candle-lit lanterns shining forth from the blessed mountain. What's more, though candles could be dangerous and cause fires in other places from time to time, the luck of Zhishan seemed to protect the people who lived on the mountain from such fires. No fire ever broke out on Zhishan at the time of the Festival of Lights. The area right around Zhishan, though, was not so fortunate. Strangely enough, every time lanterns were hung on Zhishan, fire did break out from some other source in the Meng Jia (today's Wan

Li) area of Shilin. This area that lay just below the mountain went up in flames from some sudden and destructive fire every time lanterns were hung up on the mountain of Zhishan.

People who determine the lucky locations, and those locations best suiting the natural surroundings, for homes, temples, and other buildings are know as geomancers. Geomancers in Shilin determined that the fires occurred because conditions on Zhishan affected the Meng Jia area beneath it. Although bats in the caves of Zhishan protected people living on the mountain from an outbreak of fire, the presence of fire-lit candles on Zhishan affected Meng Jia in a different way. Something in the interaction of conditions on Zhishan and the surrounding Meng Jia area seemed to determine a different response to the particular placement of the lanterns. Unless a way could be found to break up this pattern, terrible fires would continue to occur in the area around Zhishan.

One way to break up the pattern was to change the roadways along which lanterns were hung, bats flew, and people traveled up the mountainside. So it was that a geomancer was commissioned by the people of Meng Jia to recommend what should be done. This geomancer said to the people who lived on Zhishan, "The cemetery atop this mountain is a wonder to behold. The sight of bats flying forth from nearby caves is magnificent. How unfortunate, though, that the road leading to the gravesites is too narrow. It is difficult for people to get to the cemetery. It would be a good idea to widen the road to make passage more convenient." The purpose of the geomancer, working as he was for the residents of Meng Jia, was to change some condition on Zhishan that would alter the existing pattern of things. In this way, he and his clients hoped to end the fires to which Meng Jia had been susceptible.

The residents on Zhishan went along with the geomancer's suggestion. The road leading to the beautiful cemetery atop the mountain was widened, making transportation more convenient. But in altering the existing pattern in such a way as to benefit the people in Meng Jia, those widening the road destroyed the good *fengshui* of Zhishan itself. The alteration of the roadway confused the bats, who depended on the old narrow pathway to lead them toward the caves which surrounded the cemetery. The number of bats living in the caves dropped dramatically, and then the good luck creatures disappeared completely. And without the presence of the good-luck bats, Zhishan lost the air of excellent fortune it had enjoyed for many centuries.

Questions for Discussion

1. You don't have to accept all of the beliefs about *fengshui* to understand that the precise location and placement of things can affect both the natural environment and the people who live and move within that environment. What are some of the ways, for example, that your life is affected by where your home is located? How is your life affected by the location of your bedroom? By furniture placement in your room?

2. In this story, and in Taiwanese culture, bats are symbols of good luck. Why? In our society, bats have been considered a nuisance. Why? Do you think that bats are lucky or unlucky? Explain.

3. In this story the people of Zhishan Mountain sacrifice their good luck so that the people of Mengjia would not have such bad luck. Do we ever make sacrifices so that others in the community, the country, or the world might have a better life? Cite examples, if you can.

Suggestions for Class Activities

1. Offer your class the opportunity to rearrange your room in some way. This could, at your discretion, involve minor or fundamental changes in the way your room is arranged. Encourage the class to think through carefully how the changes that the students propose will alter the classroom environment and people's attitudes.

2. Have the students research bats, then write a report about them. What types of bats might there be in Taiwan? Does the research lead any students to revise their thinking about whether bats are lucky or unlucky?

3. Ask students to find maps of Taiwan in the library or on the Internet. Do these maps show mountains? Can they find Zhishan? Can they find Taibei?

Twenty-One

Have you ever set up a lemonade stand? Here is a true story of a Taiwanese girl who put up a stand to sell a most unusual and tasty drink discovered by her father.

The Origins of Aiyu

Every year as summer draws near, peddlers in rural Taiwan set up carts and stands along the road selling all kinds of iced drinks. One of the drinks that they sell is made from a frozen type of iced fruit, pale yellow in color, cool, and tasty. The frozen concoction seems to melt as soon as it hits the mouth. Most people call the icy treat Aiyu Ice or, sometimes, simply Aiyu. Aiyu means "Love Jade" to Mandarin speakers in Taiwan. Aiyu is made in Dapu District of Jiayi County. The Taiwanese tell a special story about how this cold drink came to be named Aiyu.

It is said that many years ago there was a businessperson who traveled around to the various villages in the mountains around Jiayi to conduct his business. One day he passed through today's Dapu District. Traveling in the southern part of Taiwan in the summertime is no easy task. The sun shines down incessantly, except on those days when rains brought by typhoons cloud the skies and flood the fields. The businessperson seized the opportunity to take a break from his labors when he saw a tree that offered abundant shade beside a freshwater stream. The man reached into the stream and drew a big gulp of what he assumed would be pure, clear liquid into his cupped hands. But the stream was laden with chunks of ice, coming into his hands and mouth as round, supple pieces soon landing cool and tasty on his thankful tongue. When he held the icy stuff in his mouth, the taste that came through was exceedingly fine, fragrant to the nostrils, fresh on the tongue, a most pleasing treat for the senses. As he sat there holding the icy treat in his mouth and still wondering at the extraordinary taste, there suddenly dropped from the tree a bit of fruit, falling on a stone in the stream. A thick fluid came oozing from the fruit deep into the stream. In a twinkling of the eye, the fruit's juice froze, and the businessperson had a surge of insight. Kneeling in front of the tree, he said, "Much thanks to you, Heaven Above, for sending me fruit so rare in this wide, wide, world."

Thereafter the businessperson grabbed up a bundle of this fruit to carry toward home. He took the inner part of the fruit in his hands and carefully gave it a washing, adding a bit of sugar water. The final version of the man's concoction became an icy treat, very fruity, with just the right burst of sweetness.

Now this businessperson had a nine-year-old daughter by the name of Aiyu, a beautiful and clever child. One day, instead of playing the usual games and sports with her friends, Aiyu took the drink her father had invented out by the side of the road that ran near their village. She joined the other peddlers selling their drinks to thirsty summer travelers, who thought she looked so very cute, this small salesperson taking her place beside adult and adolescent peddlers. They almost fell over themselves in their haste to purchase her drink.

"Aiyu, please give me a bowl," a villager to her left would say, while to her right another said the very same thing: "Aiyu, please give me a bowl." As the years passed, people came to call this iced fruit Aiyu Ice in honor of the pretty and industrious girl who popularized the sweet-tasting concoction invented by her equally clever father.

Questions for Discussion

1. Have you ever made a surprise discovery that turned out to be wonderful? Tell your classmates about this experience and listen to their tales of similar occurrences.

2. One theme of this story is the importance of recognizing an opportunity when it comes to you. Describe an opportunity you have had that you recognized and of which you took advantage. Did it make your life or the lives of others better?

3. If you could invent something, what would it be, and what would you call it? Would you like an invention to be named for you? If so, what invention would you most like to bear your name?

Suggestions for Class Activities

1. Taking care to encourage reasonable and healthful suggestions, have the class discuss new beverages or dishes that might be invented, using natural ingredients such as fruit, juices, and ice, perhaps combined in a blender. Have students decide the precise ingredients that they would like to use, the proportions of each ingredient that should go in the concoction, and what they would like to name their invention. Then set aside time to put the concoction together and try it.

2. Ask students to make a list of problems, such as mosquito bites or tangles in the hair. When they've finished their lists, have them think of an invention that might be used to solve one of the problems, and then either write a description of the invention or illustrate it in a drawing.

3. Conduct an experiment designed to demonstrate whether a fruit, say, a plum or a mango, can actually turn to ice in water that is not frozen solid. Find out how cold the water has to be to freeze fruit, if indeed this is possible in water that is not completely frozen. As part of the investigation, have the students research, in the library and on the Internet, the nature of this fruit called Aiyu. Do we have this fruit or anything close to it in the United States? Have the students write up the results of their experiment and their investigation into the nature of Aiyu.

Twenty-Two

Do you have heroines or heroes who are a part of your life right now? Are there people whom everyone in the United States regards as a heroine or hero? The Taiwanese sometimes develop so much respect for particular heroines and heroes that they eventually build temples in their honor. Here is the story of one such hero.

The Trials and Triumphs of General Chen-Fu

At the midpoint of the eighteenth century, a terrible famine brought misery to hundreds of people in central Taiwan. During such times, desperate people turned to robbery and theft in their attempts to ensure the survival of their children, their families, and themselves. Those who were already given to a life of crime continued to prey on the unfortunate. Under such conditions, the lives of the people of the region grew more desperate with each passing day.

Even under ordinary conditions, Taiwan at this time was a wild and dangerous frontier. It was controlled by the Qing dynasty, and this imperial government of China sent magistrates to govern the island on behalf of the dynasty. These officials were stationed one hundred miles from the Chinese southeastern coast, however, and hundreds of miles from the imperial Chinese capital of Beijing. The Qing dynasty magistrates were natives of other places in China, they had been educated on the mainland and aspired to other positions in government that would be closer to the places of their birth, education, and social interaction. They did not want to be in Taiwan.

There were others, however, who very much wanted to be in Taiwan—people whose families had been established on the island for many decades. These were people of wealth, power, and influence, people who owned a great deal of land, ate well, and wore fine clothes. These people had to obey the laws of the Qing dynasty that the magistrates were sent to Taiwan to enforce, but the magistrates had to depend on these locally powerful people to help them keep order in rural Taiwan. These wealthy families often kept their own militia (private soldiers) to guard against robbers, thieves, and murderers. If these large, landowning families so chose, they could be of great help to the Qing dynasty officials. In times of relative peace, they could help the government keep this condition. In times of natural disaster or rebellion, they could help the government steer things back toward a more peaceful way of life.

To secure the cooperation of these locally powerful families, Qing dynasty officials often relaxed tax collections and in other ways made lives for the already comfortable even more so. This placed a greater burden on the poorer people, who continued to pay high portions of their income in tax and rent. When conditions of drought, flood, or famine hit the countryside, the poor's normally difficult circumstances became all the more desperate.

Every once in while, though, a person of power and determination rose up to address the plight of the poor and to help them improve their situation in the face of the coalition of the government and the wealthy. The Daoist (Taoist) religion of Taiwan holds such people in high regard. People who perform particularly notable service in the cause of improving people's lives in time may be honored as a god worthy of worship in a temple dedicated especially to them. Such was the case with General Chen-fu.

"Chen-fu" is actually a name of honor that was eventually bestowed on this hero. His original name was Chen Muozhang, a wealthy person from the Yuanlin district of central Taiwan. He was that good kind of wealthy person who also lived in Taiwan, someone more concerned with making the lives of the people better than with further enriching himself. He was frequently disgusted with government magistrates and those of his own social station who conspired to benefit themselves at the expense of the poor.

During the rough times of the mid–eighteenth century, General Chen-fu opened his personal granary (a place where rice and other grain crops are stored until they are sold) to feed the starving people of the area. He also led his soldiers to the homes of the wealthy landowners of the region and commanded them to open up their own granaries and to contribute to a fund for the relief of the poor. He told them, "Have you not more than you need? Cannot you feed your family for many months and even years to come with the grain that you have stored? Do you not have enough money to buy all that you need, with much left over for fine robes and works of art and furniture produced by the most skilled craftspeople? Why, then, should the people starve? You will help me help these people in need, or my soldiers will make your lives very much more difficult."

The wealthy folk had no choice but to agree to General Chen-fu's demands. He was a person of strength and conviction. His loyal soldiers would enforce his policies in behalf of the poor. But even as they agreed to his demands, these locally wealthy and influential people worked to bring about General Chen-fu's downfall. They took their complaints about the good general to those who gave them a ready ear: the officials of the Qing dynasty who served in the district.

Their friend the magistrate responded immediately. He gathered Qing dynasty forces stationed on Taiwan, together with several private militia of his allies among the large landowners. These combined forces marched to the home of General Chen-fu and overwhelmed his soldiers, who were among the best and most disciplined on Taiwan but were simply unable to overcome the sheer numbers of their opposition. The magistrate had General Chen-fu arrested and brought before him. There had been no proper investigation, and there would be no proper trial. There would be only the words of the magistrate that determined the fate of General Chen-fu, and his destiny: "General Chen-fu, the Qing empire recognizes your past service and thanks you for your many demonstrations of bravery in defending the representatives of the dynasty. How much more disappointing it is, then, that I now must find you guilty of stirring up rebellion among the people. I must find you guilty, therefore, of treason, and as you know I have no alternative but to sentence you to death for an offense this serious." The magistrate wrote a message to the stout commander who had led the charge onto General Chen-fu's property, against those who had helped the general assist the people with food and other items of relief. The commander read the message, nodded, then signaled to those in the room and under his authority to seize General Chen-fu and then follow him outside.

Once outside, General Chen-fu suffered one of the most terrible fates imaginable for the Taiwanese. The Taiwanese hold the human body as sacred, a vessel to be treated with respect and dignity in the service of the ancestors and all of those who come after in the family's future generations. Bodily mutilation and violent deaths are cause for much dread and fear. Yet this was to be General Chen-fu's fate: The soldiers of the Qing tied each arm and each leg to a different strong and swift horse. The horses were then made to run at full speed, each in a different direction. General Chen-fu's body was brutally torn apart. He was then given an equally shameful and hasty burial.

The folk who had been the recipients of General Chen-fu's benevolence erected a temple in his honor. They worshiped him in this temple as a god. Day after day, month after month, year after year, people came to the temple in honor of the man who had done so much to relieve their suffering. They would enter the temple and place on an altar food, drink, paper money, and other gifts that they thought would make General Chen-fu comfortable, wealthy, and happy in the afterlife. The individual worshipers would light incense, bow deeply, and utter words of praise and comfort to their fallen hero: "Oh, General Chen-fu, I remember how you helped my family, friends, and me in our time of need. I offer these gifts and my words of praise to you now in your own time of trial. May my humble offerings be of help to you and make your life better in the world that you were forced to enter before the natural span of your life had run its course. None of us will ever forget your many kindnesses, your brave deeds, and your efforts to make our lives bearable. Thank you, honorable sir, for all that you have done. May your time in the world beyond this one be filled with peace and prosperity."

And so this kind of worshipful tribute to the life of General Chen-fu continued for many, many years. But then in one year, there came a natural disaster, one of the many to which Taiwan is frequently subjected. A great flood sent waters flowing over fields, against homes, and through temples and other buildings. The temple to General Chen-fu was among the structures destroyed. His greatest supporters, the poor of the district, grieved terribly, all the more because they had again fallen on such hard times that they could not properly do honor to their hero. They had no money to secure the materials to properly rebuild the temple. Nor were the months ahead any kinder. Drought and famine followed as one disaster replaced another. The very conditions that General Chen-fu had worked so hard to help them endure now made repairing the temple in his honor impossible.

Then, many years later, in a district in Nantou county, a doctor by the name of Xu Wanqi had a series of experiences that led to a new effort in the service of General Chen-fu's memory. First, a peasant uprising threatened the fortunes of the doctor's friends among the rich and powerful. These friends called upon Dr. Xu to help them feed, clothe, and arm the forces necessary to put down the rebellion. Dr. Xu complied with the request of his friends, whose forces did, in a matter of days, end the rebellion. Many of these rebels suffered the kind of fate that General Chen-fu had endured at the end of his life: They were drawn, quartered, and pulled asunder to the thundering sound of the hooves of swift horses.

Soon after these events, Dr. Xu had a disturbing dream. An old man puffing a pipe, smoke enveloping his thick mane of white hair, came forward in the dream and stared right into Dr. Xu's eyes. The glare was intense, the old man's eyes penetrating, the tone of his voice full of righteous indignation. The old man spoke thus to Dr. Xu: "Why do you seek to harm my people?" Having uttered that simple but troubling question, the old man rapped Dr. Xu on his left foot with his pipe and vanished as quickly as he had appeared.

Dr. Xu woke from his dream, finding himself rubbing a very sore left foot. He thought it odd that his physical state should so closely correspond to the blow that the old man had given him in his dream. But he told himself that nevertheless this had just been a dream. He must not, he said to himself, overreact. He would be fine. The throbbing in his left foot was simply a strange coincidence.

Then the next night Dr. Xu found the white-haired old man once more dominating his dreams and disturbing his sleep. Tugging on his pipe, he spoke to Dr. Xu in the same sturdy voice: "I am Chen Mozhuang, whom many have known as General Chen-fu. Please rebuild my temple, so that I may once again hear the prayers of my people and give them what service I can." This time there was no rap with the pipe, just a quick exit. But if anything, the tone, the gaze, and the request had left Dr. Xu feeling more disturbed than he had after his earlier dream.

The temple to General Chen-fu had long since crumbled and only a few people in the area still held his memory close in their hearts. Dr. Xu himself had known nothing of General Chen-fu, nor had he heard tell of anyone named Chen Mozhuang. He conducted an investigation, though, among the people of the region and in the records of the county government. His research showed that such a person had indeed existed. Soon, Dr. Xu located the remains of the temple dedicated to General Chen-fu. Out of a sense of shame for his past deeds that had made the lives of the poor more difficult, and out of respect for the old man in his dreams, Dr. Xu dedicated a large portion of his substantial resources to the rebuilding of the temple.

Those who had kept the memory of General Chen-fu alive in their hearts and at the altars of their own homes came to the temple. They told others about the deeds of the general and about the dreams of Dr. Xu. The following of General Chen-fu grew steadily larger as the years passed. People came to revere him for his benevolent ways and to pray for blessings in their lives. When natural disaster struck, they would ask him for assistance. Their prayers seemed generally to meet with positive replies and better conditions. So the incense burned in honor of General Chen-fu continued to fill his temple with sweet smells that flowed skyward in his honor. To this day, his temple has been kept in top condition, and he has not been forgotten.

Questions for Discussion

1. Why did people who lived in General Chen-fu's own time, as well as those who lived in later times, come to regard him as a hero? Would his personal qualities and deeds have made him a hero to you?

2. Are there people in your own life right now whom you consider heroines or heroes? Who are they, and what traits make them heroes or heroines in your eyes?

3. Who are the people whom most people in the United States seem to regard as heroines or heroes today? What are the ways in which the nation honors such people? Compare the way in which Americans and Taiwanese honor heroines and heroes, and share some reasons that might explain the differences.

Suggestions for Class Activities

1. After having discussed the qualities of heroism suggested in the discussion questions, have each student write an essay in which she or he chooses one person who best fits that student's ideal of what a heroine or hero should be, explaining in detail why that person fits that ideal. Follow this up with a class discussion focused on student ideas of heroism as reflected in their essays, making a list on the board showing the heroic traits that seem important to people in the class.

2. Have students prepare a two-media presentation in which they paint, draw, or make a sculpture of a person frequently considered a national hero and then pair this artistic rendering with a personally written text explaining why and how the nation honors the person they selected. Have the students explain their art and text to the class in a well- prepared oral presentation.

3. Conduct research on the temples of Taiwan in the library and on the Internet. Can you find any information about the temple of General Chen-fu?

4. Does Taiwan have a military today? Conduct research on the Internet and in the library to find out and discuss findings.

Twenty-Three

Have you ever looked deep down into a well and wondered what lay at the bottom? Here is the story of some Taiwanese people who did so—and got a big surprise.

The Red-Haired Well

Three hundred years ago, when the Dutch controlled Taiwan, they extended their rule to the area around today's city of Chiayi. In the area where the south gate of the city still lies, the Dutch rulers of Chiayi drilled a well. The Han Taiwanese who lived and worked under the Dutch referred to their colonial overlords as the "Red-haired Men," a term that these Taiwanese often used for all Westerners. With the builders in mind, the Taiwanese people who lived in Chiayi named the well the "Red-Haired Well." The name has endured to this day.

For three hundred years after it was built, the Red-Haired Well never failed to yield water. No matter what sort of weather came to the Chiayi region, the well was always full. The Chiayi region of Taiwan is generally fertile and moist, but its people have suffered times of very hot weather when little rain fell. Even during such times, the amount of water in the Red-Haired Well never decreased. In fact, during a few of these spells of drought, its water level actually rose.

In the year 1906, an earthquake hit Chiayi, causing great flooding and the usual destruction that floods bring. All other wells in the region were severely damaged by the earthquake, but the Red-Haired Well alone continued to hold water in great abundance. Its seemingly miraculous ability to continue to hold water under conditions of earthquakes, drought, and other natural disasters at last motivated a team of investigators to try to discover the reason for the well's never-failing reliability.

Some of the investigators lowered themselves to the bottom of the well where they found a wooden plank. The members of the team pulled the plank up to find that water spewed forth in great abundance, gushing up like a fountain toward those looking down curiously from the top of the well. With a bit more investigation and analysis, the team realized that the source of this well was the sea itself! The Dutch had dug a long underground canal straight to the Taiwan Strait some fifty miles away. No wonder that the Red-Haired Well never failed. The sea itself had always been full of water, making sure that this well had water when other wells did not, whether conditions in Chiayi itself were wet or dry!

After the investigators made their discovery, people of the area began to think of a story that had often been told about the Dutch and their defeat at the hands of Koxinga. This story maintains that when Koxinga achieved his victory over the Dutch, he gave them three days to leave the island. Beyond that, any Dutch people who remained on Taiwan would be put to death. Most did evacuate the island, though it is said that those living in the Chiayi area could not get ready in time to meet Koxinga's deadline. Those left behind secretly built a tunnel and crawled through the narrow escape route to the sea. Having eluded discovery and escaped Koxinga's threatened punishment, they boarded ship for the long trip back home to the Netherlands.

The people of Chiayi now believe that the Dutch in fact dug their tunnel from the area of the Red-Haired Well and that this tunnel immediately began to carry water from the ever-abundant sea to the never-failing well that has served the city so well.

Questions for Discussion

1. Not all Dutch people have red hair, yet the Taiwanese people called the male colonizers from the Netherlands the "Red Haired Men." Why do you think this was so?

2. Every region of the world occasionally has conditions that qualify as a natural disaster, such as a flood, drought, earthquake, tornado, or hurricane. Discuss the most frequently occurring natural disaster in your region and why your area of the nation seems to be more vulnerable to this natural disaster than others.

3. In this story, what had seemed to be a miraculous well turned out to have logical reasons for its never-ending supply of water. Have you ever had something happen that at first seemed miraculous but turned out to have a perfectly logical explanation? Share your story with the class.

Suggestions for Class Activities

1. In groups of four or five, have students research the impact of the Dutch in Southeast and East Asia. Using encyclopedias, world history texts, books from the Core Knowledge Foundation, or resources on the Internet, have group members decide how to divide and assign responsibilities for answering such questions as the following:

    *   Why did the Dutch leave northern Europe to go on missions of exploration and discovery?

    *   How did their goals compare to those of other countries, such as Portugal, Spain, and Great Britain?

    *   Why might Taiwan have been a valuable colony for the Dutch, given their Southeast Asian base of operations (have students first find out where this was) and their trade with people on mainland China and Japan?

    Have the groups share the results of their investigations with the class.

2. In this story, an earthquake occurs. Conduct research in the library and on the Internet to see what you can find out about the earthquake of 1906. Have there been other earthquakes in Taiwan? Is Taiwan on a fault line? Compare the 1906 earthquake to the earthquakes in other parts of the world—for example, the San Francisco earthquake in the same year. Were causes and consequences the same?

Twenty-Four

The turtle is one of those animals that symbolize certain qualities to the Taiwanese. In this story, you'll find out what those qualities are, why a turtle was made of stone, and how it came to swim.

The Stone Turtle That Could Swim

In the days of the Qing dynasty, it was the practice of the emperors to honor dedicated officials who had helped to put down rebellions. Emperors commonly sent stone pillars inscribed with words of praise to the place where the noble deed was performed. In this way, the stone pillars and the people whom they honored might inspire other officials to follow their example. Inscriptions written on one of these stone pillars would tell the tale of the officials' glorious deeds. The stone pillars would be placed in prominent places along the streets and avenues of the cities near where the officials had performed their service to the dynasty.

Situated at the great south gate of the city of Tainan there are to this day ten such pillars erected in honor of officials who in the service of the Qing dynasty put down rebels and restored order to the region. Nine of these pillars are placed on enormous turtle-shaped stands—five feet wide, eight feet long, and three feet thick. But one of the pillars stands on a plain stone base bearing no resemblance to the form of a turtle. The stone turtle originally designated to support this tenth pillar underwent a long ordeal that ultimately landed it in a place of special honor. Here is how this happened.

In the fifty-first year of the Emperor Qianlong (1787), General Fu Kangan successfully put down one of the rebellions that seemed to rock Taiwan every three to five years. This rebellion was the most serious of them all. It was led by a man named Lin Shuangwen, whose troops for over a year caused great trouble for the Qing rulers of Taiwan. After General Fu successfully ended the great rebellion, Emperor Qianlong ordered that a pillar be carved in honor of the general's service to the dynasty and that a great stone turtle be sculpted to serve as a foundation for the pillar.

Emperor Qianlong had a fondness for these stone turtles, which are Chinese symbols of longevity, endurance, and persistence. Nine other such stone turtles would be manufactured for dynastic heroes who had served in the Tainan region. But this particular stone turtle fell victim to the turbulent Taiwan Strait while aboard ship en route from the Chinese mainland, where it had been carved. Amid high winds and crashing waves, the stone turtle intended to support the pillar dedicated to General Fu Kangan slid from its position on the ship's deck and tumbled into the sea. It quickly disappeared beneath the water. There was no way to retrieve such a heavy object, and for decades thereafter the stone turtle intended to honor the general was entirely forgotten.

One day in 1910, when Taiwan had come under Japanese control, a strange sight presented itself to a fisher sitting in his boat at Anping port, just outside the city of Tainan. The fisher had just about caught his daily quota of fish when a huge creature swam up to his boat. It was a turtle, the largest that the fisher had ever seen, much too large for one person to handle. The fisher called to a number of his friends still bringing in their daily catch, "Hey, help me bring this big thing in! It's the biggest turtle I've ever seen in my life!"

Seven fishers worked together to bring the turtle aboard. The boat rocked and dipped in response to the movement and the weight of its cargo. Then the fishers felt the boat get even heavier, even as the turtle itself grew still. The fisher who had first sighted the turtle was also the first to notice that the turtle itself had ceased to move. The creature of real meat and shell and moving legs had become as still as a creature made of stone. The fisher bent down, touched the turtle, and soon discovered why this was so: The turtle had indeed turned to stone.

In fact, this was the long-lost turtle that had fallen into the sea way back in 1789, more than a hundred years earlier. The people of Tainan came to hold this stone turtle in high regard. It had outdone all other turtles, real or stone, in the degree to which it demonstrated the traits that had so appealed to emperor Qianlong: longevity, endurance, and persistence. Originally destined for a position along with the others at the great south gate of Tainan, this turtle was given a place of even greater distinction. While the pillar that the stone turtle was originally meant to support had to make do with a plain stone base, this special stone turtle was given a place of reverence at the very front of the city's Nanchang Temple, where it sits to this day.

Questions for Discussion

1. The turtle is said by the Chinese to symbolize "longevity," "endurance," and "persistence." What does each of these terms mean, and why do you think that Chinese people consider the turtle to symbolize them?

2. People often attribute certain qualities to animals that represent personality or character traits observed in people as well. What is meant by the terms "personality trait" and "character trait"? What animals do we commonly say represent certain traits, and in each case why do we assign this trait or these traits to the particular animal?

3. Do you think that General Fu Kangan would have been as much a hero to the people of Taiwan in 1789 as he was to Emperor Qianlong? For what reasons might some people have found him to be a hero? For what reasons might some people not have considered him a hero?

Suggestions for Class Activities

1. Choose a book with animal characters to read aloud to the class, for example, Aesop's Fables, George Orwell's *Animal Farm,* or Lewis Carroll's *Alice in Wonderland.* Have the students discuss what the animals represent in the piece of literature that you choose and why they are depicted as they are.

2. Have students research turtles. What is the difference between a turtle and a tortoise? What kinds of turtles can be found in China and Taiwan today? What kinds of turtles live in your area? Have students write a report about turtles.

3. Have students research the Qing dynasty, comparing its rule on Taiwan to British rule in the United States. Are there parallels? Differences?

Twenty-Five

Many times the story behind an important institution is a mixture of legend and fact, both significant to the people who hold the institution dear. Here is a story that combines the legend and history of Longshan ("Dragon Mountain") Temple in Taiwan's capital city of Taibei.

The Legend and History of Longshan Temple

Legend has it that more than two centuries ago a merchant from Quanzhou arrived in the Chingwei area of northern Taiwan with the purpose of purchasing rattan. [Rattan is the tough stem of a palm tree found in Taiwan that is used to make wicker furniture, canes, and other items.] When he passed through the area now known as Wanhua, the merchant stopped for a rest in a plaza where dyed cloth had been stretched out to dry. After awhile, the merchant strolled toward the front door of a nearby public restroom, pulling out a bag of incense from his breast pocket as he did so. The merchant hung his bag of incense on the branch of a nearby tree, giving praise to the gods who dwelled in these woods. But after using the restroom, the merchant strolled on absentmindedly without retrieving his bag of incense.

That evening, someone noticed smoke rising from the plaza that people used to dye and dry cloth. Upon taking a closer look, the person realized that a bag of incense was hanging from the branch of one of the trees. On this bag of incense was written, "Longshan Temple, Guanyin Bodhisattva." Thereafter the people of the region came to worship this bag of incense. Through the years, devotees came in greater and greater numbers to kneel and pay their respects to Guanyin, who is revered in Taiwan as the Goddess of Mercy. In time it was agreed that the incense that had been hung from the tree carried with it an implied prophesy that a temple should be built at the spot where the merchant had hung his bag. Work began in the second year, third month, and eighteenth day of the emperor Qianlong on the construction of the place of worship to be known as Longshan Temple. The best artisans in all Taiwan were summoned to help with the construction—stone masons, woodcarvers, carpenters, painters. The temple was fully constructed in the fifth year, second month, and eighth day of Qianlong's reign.

After the temple was fully constructed, people of the Wanhua area hired a geomancer [one who determines the proper placement of human-made buildings in relation to natural surroundings] to help with the landscaping for the temple. This person, Zhang Chayuan, said that the *fengshui* [literally, "wind and water": the natural surroundings of an area, which should be taken into consideration when building houses and other objects of human construction] of the land around the temple suggested that there should be a "mirror" of some sort to reflect the image of Guanyin. Some distance from Guanyin's "Divine Den," as the geomancer called her place in the temple, there should be a reflecting pool to symbolize the reflection of divinity. So as one of their last tasks, workers at the temple dug a hole and filled it with water to form the reflecting pool in fulfillment of the specifications of the geomancer.

As the years went on, Longshan temple was damaged many times from the effects of earthquakes and floods. So severe was the damage in one of these episodes that the whole temple had to be reconstructed. During the Japanese colonial era, American bombing of the island threatened Longshan Temple again. The temple itself was once again almost totally destroyed, but in this destruction was embedded a circumstance that served to deepen the faith of those who worship Guanyin Bodhisattva. The statue of Guanyin stood unharmed amid the terrible destruction to which most of the other objects in the temple had been subjected. Guanyin's image remained calm, composed, with the same compassionate expression that she had worn throughout her years of rest in her "Divine Den."

Seeing Guanyin's statue lying flawless as the day she first entered the temple inspired the people of Wanhua to undertake another thorough reconstruction of the temple. Men and women among the faithful contributed large sums from their savings to ensure the reconstruction of Longshan Temple. About the same time the Japanese were forced to depart Taiwan at the end of World War II, the temple came to life again. Fragrant incense wafted through the temple. People kneeled, even as had the legendary merchant and his successors in the forest suspending the bag of incense that inspired the initial construction of the temple. Old men gathered to play *xiangxi*, children romped through the temple plaza playing games, musicians gathered with their gongs, drums, and stringed instruments. A wall now lay at the entrance to the shrine dedicated to Guanyin, separating her image from her reflecting pool. But the faithful landscaped the pool even more beautifully, with lush plants and a calming waterfall. The pool now mirrored the images of the faithful who peered into its waters, people whose faith has been as enduring as the statue of the Goddess of Mercy herself.

Questions for Discussion

1. Are there stores, houses, cemeteries, or places of worship in your community about which people tell stories? Are these stories made up of legend, historical events, or some combination of the two? Share stories you know about places in your community.

2. The story mentions that "stone masons, woodcarvers, carpenters, and painters" all helped to construct Longshan Temple. Think of churches, synagogues, temples, and other places of worship in your own community. Were all of these types of artisans and artists involved in the construction of those institutions? What artisans, artists, or other contributors were involved in the construction of the buildings that serve as places of worship in your community?

3. Think about examples of public art in your community. What are the messages or purposes of such art? What does the public artwork near your house say about the values or concerns of people in your community?

Suggestions for Class Activities

1. Have students discuss ways in which works of art might represent characteristics for which the class as a whole would like to be known. Divide the class into groups of four or five, with each group holding the responsibility to create a work of art that will be displayed in the class. Encourage each group to take its cue from the values or characteristics that the class as a community has identified as important.

2. The story mentions the destruction that occurred to Longshan Temple during World War II. Have students research the ways in which the Japanese occupation during World War II affected people in such places as Vietnam, Indonesia, Taiwan, Korea, and the Philippines. How did American bombing affect these countries and Japan itself? Are there temples in Taiwan today? What do they look like? What religions are common in Taiwan? Conduct research in the library and on the Internet and compare findings.

Twenty-Six

Many countries have a history of conflict between the first inhabitants and those who came later. Here is a tale that shows evidence of such conflict in Taiwan.

The Legend of Sun Moon Lake

More than two hundred years ago, several hundred Taiwanese aborigines from Alishan arrived at the spot that today is considered the most beautiful lake on the island: Sun Moon Lake. At one point these native people were chasing a white deer when by accident they happened upon this absolutely splendid body of water. Having already fallen in love with the fluffy clouds that so often magnified the beauty of the green hills ringing this lovely spot, they had very little trouble deciding to move to the shores of Sun Moon Lake.

They moved, that is, to what the Taiwanese today call Sun Moon Lake. At that time, the aborigines called the lake Big Lake Shuishe. At the lake's center lies a small island they named after the precious gift of the oyster: They called it Pearl Island, though today it is know as Guanghua ("Radiant") Island. This island divides the lake into two halves, a northern part shaped like the sun, and a southern part shaped like the new moon. This is how the lake got its current name of Sun Moon Lake.

It is said that not long after the aborigines settled in this region, a tree sprouted up from the depths of the northeastern portion of the lake. Rooted to the lake's bottom, the tree grew to a height of more than ten kilometers. One day the Tree God cast its essence into the body of an aborigine woman, who in the aftermath gave birth to a very special boy. As soon as the baby emerged from his mother's womb, he grew to a height of six feet. His face soon sprouted a full-length, flowing beard. He matured rapidly and proved to be a man of extraordinary leadership ability. Soon he claimed the title of chief, and no one contested him for the title. Unfortunately, he ruled the surrounding area with an iron hand and proved also to have a cruel nature. He was unkind to his own people, but he was especially tough on any Han Taiwanese who dared enter his domain.

These circumstances drew the attention of the Qing dynasty's inspector-general of the time, Wu Changzuo. Inspector-General Wu dispatched an army, well-armed and with orders to capture the tyrant chieftain. But the chief was much too strong for this Qing force and turned the invaders back with little difficulty. After being thoroughly beaten, the Qing army beat a hasty retreat.

The actions of the chief continued to plague his own people, and they became more and more aggressive toward all Han Taiwanese. One day, an adviser to the inspector general suggested a solution: A copper needle smeared with dog's blood would be injected into the magical tree that had invested the chieftain with its powerful spirit. The tree should then be severed at the base of its trunk, severing in turn the power of the tree spirit. If the solution of dog's blood worked as the adviser said it would, the tree would be weakened enough to allow cutting, and the rest of the plan would unfold as he predicted. Because no one else had a better idea, Inspector-General Wu decided to give this plan a try. He sent attendants to prepare the necessary materials, then charged several other underlings with the task of injecting the solution and severing the tree.

The inspector-general's group crept stealthily toward a spot along Sun Moon Lake nearest the sacred tree. Beating back the fear that pounded in their hearts, they slipped into boats and pulled alongside Pearl Island. They climbed out of their boats and approached the tree. Working with copper needle and saws, they fulfilled their tasks, first injecting the dog's blood into the tree, then cutting the powerful tree in two.

The huge tree fell with tremendous force into the lake, producing waves so high as to make a surfer yelp in delight. More important to the representatives of the Qing dynasty's Inspector-General Wu, though, the magic spirit inside the sacred tree oozed from the cut made by the saws. Not far away the chieftain who had drawn his power from the spiritual essence of the great tree lay sleeping on Pearl Island. He awoke to the crash of the tree and the roar of the waves. He stood up, but he was not as he had been before taking his slumber. His arms and legs felt weak, and his head was light. He felt none of the power or confidence that had made him such a strong and terrible leader. With anguish rising from his heart and his spirit drifting out of his body, the formerly powerful man jumped to his doom in Sun Moon Lake.

The descendants of the fallen leader, the Tsou aboriginal people, continue to live in the area that they discovered two centuries ago. While they have been rid of the powerful son of the tree spirit for these many years, they themselves continue to confront the problem of living in harmony with the Han Taiwanese. They have come to understand the frustrations that may have intensified the cruel nature of the great chieftain who led their people two hundred years ago. But they have committed to peaceful solutions in their quest for dignity and inclusion among the diverse people who together are known as the Taiwanese.

Questions for Discussion

1. What can you imagine were the "frustrations that may have intensified the cruel nature of the great chieftain"?

2. In an ideal world, would native people forever have the main claim to land they reached before all others? How would you relate your answer to similar questions about the rights of Native American people in the United States or other parts of the Americas?

3. Does this seem more like a tale told and cherished by the aboriginal people, or by the Han people who settled Taiwan later? Explain.

Suggestions for Class Activities

1. The sacred tree of this story is inhabited by a magical and powerful spirit. Animists (people who believe that spirits dwell within objects of nature) in many lands have believed in the power of such spirits. Have the students conduct individual research projects on the animistic traditions from Japan, Africa, and Native American traditions. Have them share their discoveries with each other, comparing their findings for similarities and differences in the way nature spirits are perceived.

2. Have the students exercise their imaginations by constructing their own mental images of spirits associated with rocks, trees, streams, or other items of nature. Have each student share her or his creative image with the other students, and then have them each write a short story, poem, or song about the spirit that she or he has created.

3. This story mentions a white deer. Do such creatures live in Taiwan today? What do you suppose a white deer symbolizes? Conduct research in the library and on the Internet to find the answers to these questions.

Part Six

Taiwanese Humor

Twenty-Seven

Some people have a hard time avoiding misunderstandings and embarrassing situations. Here is a story that the Taiwanese tell about such a boy.

The Goofiness of Chen Ah Ai

Long ago there was a boy who bore the nickname of Ah Ai. His family name was Chen. One day Chen Ah Ai's mother bought him a white piece of cloth. Unfortunately, the cloth was stolen the very next day. Chen Ah Ai could not stand to be separated from the dear bolt of cloth that his mother had so lovingly purchased for him. He resolved to search everywhere until he found it. In the course of his search, Chen Ah Ai bumbled into a neighboring village. A gong and drum sounded not too far in the distance. It was the gong and drum of a funeral procession, all the mourners of which were decked out in the customary robes of white.

Chen Ah Ai screamed, "Hey! Why did you steal my stuff?" All of the mourners shot Chen Ah Ai irritated glances. Several of them gathered around the boy with raised fists. Three people in this angry crowd gave Chen Ah Ai several stiff raps on the head.

When Chen Ah Ai returned home, he tearfully told his father about the incident.

His father instructed him, "Ah Ai, you should be able to recognize a funeral procession when you see one. The people you made so angry were friends and family members of a person who died recently. From now on when you see such mourners, you should be very gentle and do nothing to disrupt their ceremony. If you speak anything at all, you should console them by saying, "How sad you must be! Please don't be so heavy of heart!"

On the very next day, Chen Ah Ai again ran into the neighboring village to look for his beloved cloth. Again he heard the sound of gong and drum. Another procession was in motion, although it looked a bit different. People were following the sedan chair being transported on the shoulders of several strong young men. Inside, a young woman, veiled and dressed in red, kept her gaze looking forward. Most Taiwanese would recognize this as a procession transporting the young woman to the village of her betrothed husband for the wedding ceremony. But all that Chen Ah Ai could think of was the gong and drum. Then he thought of the words that his father had so recently instructed him to say, "Oh, how sad you must be! Please don't be so heavy of heart!" The members of the crowd shook with rage. Several of them gave Chen Ah Ai his second thrashing in two days.

Chen Ah Ai ran home crying, eliciting from his father more words of instruction: "Those were wedding celebrants bringing a young bride to the village of the groom. You should have exclaimed, 'Congratulations!' On such occasions, your words and face should properly express your joy in the happiness of the celebrants."

Several days later, Chen Ah Ai went into the district town to spend a few hours of leisure. Soon he saw smoke wafting through the air. A crowd gathered around. Everyone was moving about in a great commotion. Not one to make very fine distinctions, but wanting to join in the action, Chen searched his brain for words to speak. All he could think of was his father's most recent instruction. He rushed forward, not realizing that a disastrous fire had struck and that all of those running around were madly trying to put out the fire. Chen Ah Ai in his ignorance shouted, "Congratulations! Congratulations!" And once again he was forced to retreat under angry blows from his fellows.

Seeing the downcast look on the face of his hapless son, Chen Ah Ai's father said, "My son, my son, what am I going to do with you? When a fire breaks out in the home of a family, all of the villagers move quickly to try to get the fire under control. It is definitely better under such circumstances to say as little as possible. People need action in such situations, not words. You should help them put out the fire!"

And so Chen Ah Ai went forth again to stroll the streets, coming in time to a blacksmith pounding away at his trade. Chen Ah Ai reckoned the smoke that rose around him from the blacksmith's fire was the sort of disaster of which his father had spoken, so he took a pail, dipped it in a tub of water, and poured it abundantly on the roaring fire. The blacksmith unleashed his furor upon Chen Ah Ai. Wearing fresh bruises, the startled young man ran out of the blacksmith's shop. He cried all the way home. When would he ever do something right and appropriate to the occasion?

Father shook his head in despair, saying, "That was the smoke of a black-smith, not a fire out of control! You not only failed to help, you put out the fire that makes a blacksmith's labor effective. You needn't wonder why he turned on you in anger!"

On yet another day, Chen Ah Ai discovered a couple of people arguing loudly about something. Thinking of how his father had told him to help others in time of need, he broke in between the two having the argument and started to fight right along with them. This only earned him a bloody nose and swollen eye to take home to his thoroughly exasperated father.

Father sighed as if at wit's end and said, "In such a situation, you should, of course, mediate the dispute. Why in the world would you jump in and start fight-ing with them? How could you think that that would be in any way helpful?"

Gravely fearful that his foolish son would again stir up trouble, Chen Ah Ai's father forbade him from that day forward to seek amusement anywhere outside his immediate neighborhood. And so it was that one day Chen Ah Ai sat on the lawn in front of his house passing time. Two water buffalo sauntered up. In time, the two beasts seemed to get angry with each other. Soon they were butting heads and nastily fighting each other. Thinking of how his father had told him to help mediate disputes, Chen Ah Ai jumped into the middle of the fight. He began to of-fer his counsel, but before he had finished his would-be helpful talk, one of the water buffaloes had struck him with a heavy blow, and he fell to the ground.

Slow to learn his lessons from either father or his fellow human beings, it re-mained to be seen whether the foolish Chen Ah Ai could learn them from a couple of water buffalo. What do you think?

Questions for Discussion

1. People in Taiwan wear white at the time of a funeral. What do people in the United States wear? What might account for this difference?

2. Brides in Taiwan wear red at the time of their wedding. What do brides in the United States wear? What do you think the colors symbolize in each society?

3. What is truly the best thing to do when two people are arguing, as happened in one circumstance that Chen Ah Ai encountered in this story?

Suggestions for Classroom Activities

1. Have the students write poems or essays on a chosen color, for example, "Red is . . ." (Note: This might be a chance to explain why white and black, although commonly referred to in the same context as colors, are not technically considered colors). After students have finished the assignment, discuss the use of symbols in literature and in life.

2. Water buffaloes are found in many countries. Have students research this animal, where it lives, and how it is used, and then have each student write a report.

3. There are many folk stories about foolish characters and noodleheads. Have students research folklore collections to find some of them and then read them aloud to the class.

Twenty-Eight

We love people for lots of reasons, and sometimes despite their faults. Here's a tale of a rather goofy guy, whose wife loved him very much, in spite of his goofiness.

A Thoroughly Goofy Son-in-Law

There was once a young man who set out with a fine red curtain, a number of ducks, and traditional good-luck noodles to present at the birthday of his father-in-law. As he walked with his gifts past a lake, the ducks that he was carrying emitted a "wah-wah" sort of a sound, which the young man interpreted to mean that they were thirsty. He carried the ducks to the water's edge so that they might get a drink, but he was careless in holding them too lightly. In the twinkling of an eye, they were gone, their wings flapping happily as they half-swam, half-flew across the lake. "Oh, well," the foolish young man thought, "maybe I'll find something to replace those ducks that will be just as good a present for father-in-law."

He soon saw something that gave him the notion that he had found a suitable replacement. A school of carp swam by in the same lake that had offered escape to the ducks. The young man thought, "It'd be a good enough trade-off if I could catch some of those carp to replace those ducks that swam away." The young man looked around and noticed that a fisher's net lay just a few yards away. "Good luck," he thought, "just like these good-luck carp!" The young man took the good-luck noodles and dangled them before the carp as if to entice them into the net. But the noodles broke apart as soon as they hit the water, floating away, then down toward lake bottom. The foolish son-in-law now had no ducks, no noodles, and no carp.

As the foolish son-in-law walked on, the sound of "hua-hua" from nearby bamboo caught his attention. "Poor bamboo!" he thought. "They must be very cold. The air is damp and cool today, and the poor bamboo are groaning so." The good-hearted, if foolish, lad took the red curtain and spread it on the bamboo, only to see the wind take the curtain and carry it out of sight. He now had no ducks, no noodles, no carp, and no fine red curtain.

Yet the young man walked on, in time coming to spy a large number of flies swarming around a pile of ox dung. As he drew near, the flies dispersed, and the foolish son-in-law thought, "The flies seem fascinated by this stuff: Perhaps I should grab up some of it." And so he did, smelling much worse now than he had when he began his journey to his father-in-law's birthday party.

As he moved on, the young man came to a farmer's house. He saw someone repairing a lunch basket that said on one side, "New basket, old basket, and so the days drift away." Thinking this some wise and profound saying, the young man committed these words to memory, resolving to impress people with his wisdom. Then, he continued his journey.

In time the young man came to a river. As he was crossing the bridge, he heard an old man sitting on the shore say, "The waves of the river lap the same, but the color of the water varies." The young man said to himself, "Now, I wonder what that means? The man is old and must be full of wisdom. I'll memorize this as another saying with which to impress the guests at father-in-law's birthday party." And again, he walked on.

At last the foolish son-in-law came to his father-in-law's house, where a room full of guests greeted him with utmost courtesy. The young man felt pressed to say something in reply and blurted out with, "Flies like the taste of cow dung, so I tried some too!" The guests' expressions turned to half-amusement and half-astonishment: They really didn't know whether to laugh or cry.

When as the meal began the foolish son-in-law discovered that all of the chopsticks placed at the table were ivory and that only he was using old bamboo chopsticks, he quickly boomed out with, "New basket, old basket, and so the days drift away." Confused, but hearing how elegantly the young man spoke these words, everyone agreed that he should be given the sort of ivory chopsticks that everyone else was using. His bamboo chopsticks were exchanged for ivory ones.

During the party, someone pulled a lousy trick on the young man, giving him a glass of cheap liquor. When he realized what the person had done to him, he decided it was the time to pull out one of those expressions that he had learned on the way to the party. Without thinking too very hard about what he was doing, the foolish son-in-law spoke thus: "The waves of the river lap the same, but the color of the water varies." Once again the young man's words stunned the crowd. Some of them thought that they understood enough of the intent of the message to swap the young man's glass of low-grade liquor for the high-quality kind that everyone else had been served.

Meanwhile, the wife of the foolish son-in-law lived in constant fear that her husband would do something embarrassing. She had worried for weeks about what he was likely to do at her father's birthday party, especially when it came time to eat dinner. The young man had a terrific appetite and frequently gorged himself when an abundance of food was set before him. But at other times, he became so distracted over something that someone had said or done that he would forget to eat entirely. His wife feared that he might offend her father and the other guests, either gobbling food or insulting the host by altogether ignoring the feast her father had arranged.

The young wife had ultimately decided on a scheme that she hoped would help her husband eat with proper manners. Just before the guests were to gather for the feast, she tied a thread to her husband's foot, then looped the other end of the thread to her own wrist. The young woman then instructed her husband, "If you feel the thread tugging on your foot, that will be my signal to you that you should eat a bite." The young man had come to trust that his wife's plans usually worked out better than his own, so he agreed to become something of a puppet on her string.

The plan worked beautifully for awhile. At first the young man ate with very good manners, consuming neither too much nor too little. But then an unforeseen event occurred. A little doggy playfully scooted under the table and got the thread wound around its paw. This scared the little animal so badly that it ran, jumped, and kicked this way and that, all around the dining room floor. The thread went into the same erratic motion, pulling constantly this way and that on the foolish son-in-law's foot. Ever obedient to his wife's instructions, the young man began to eat furiously, slamming down morsel after morsel of food. But the thread kept pulling and pulling, faster and faster, and the young man simply could not keep up. Thinking that the next best thing would be to stuff all of the food somewhere, the foolish son-in-law began to cram large portions of the feast into his pockets and under his hat. This sent everyone at the feast falling over the table or out of their chairs in loud, uncontrollable laughter.

Thus losing face before the entire crowd, the young man's wife went crazy with shame. She barged out of the house with the full intention of jumping in a pond to drown herself. When she came to the pond, though, she saw a man using a kind of rice scooping tool called a *fanlo,* on top of which rested a sieve. Watching him dip the device into the water, she forgot about her plan to end her life. With great curiosity, the young wife stepped forward and asked, "May I ask you what you are doing?"

"I dropped a needle that my wife entrusted to me into the pond, so I'm using this sieve to help me retrieve it."

Now the young wife thought to herself, "How could I have ever thought that there would in the whole world be a husband more foolish that my own? And yet mine has never done anything so outlandish as this. Maybe my husband isn't the brightest man in the world, but he's one of the best-hearted people on the planet. That should be all I need to know about him."

Any thoughts of taking her own life flew away in the wind of this realization. She lived happily with her foolish but kindhearted husband to the end of her days.

Questions for Discussion

1. What's the goofiest thing that you've ever done? Would you be willing to share this with the class, if others will, too? If so, have a goofy-true-story session.

2. Noodles are long and represent long life to the Taiwanese, as noted in the story. In Mandarin Chinese, the word for fish has the same pronunciation as that for abundance, so at the New Year every family eats a fish, leaving just a little uneaten to symbolize the coming year of plenty and prosperity. Discuss customs and symbolism associated with holiday and other meals in the United States. Do we have special dishes and foods that symbolize abundance?

3. The young wife in this story rushed out of her father's house in great mental distress, but what she saw and observed at the pond completely changed the way she thought about her situation. Have you ever seen or observed something that so completely changed the way you felt or thought? Share these experiences with each other.

Suggestions for Class Activities

1. Have each student write down the funniest true story that she or he has ever heard, or in which she or he was personally a participant. Have students practice telling these stories in small groups, and then ask for volunteers to tell their stories to the class.

2. Watch such slapstick artists as the Marx Brothers, Lucille Ball, and even the Three Stooges to have fun, but also as a vehicle for discussing what makes comedy slapstick and which techniques make it funny. Have students practice slapstick routines in small groups, then ask for volunteers to present these routines to the class.

Recipes

Note: Unless otherwise indicated, the term "pepper" in these recipes means black pepper. Full names are given for other kinds of pepper, such as crushed red pepper.

Twice-Cooked Pork

Ingredients

- ✓ 10 crushed red pepper pieces
- ✓ 5 slices of precooked ham, medium length and width
- ✓ 1 green, red, or yellow pepper
- ✓ 1 tsp. chili garlic sauce
- ✓ 1/2 tsp. salt
- ✓ 1/8 tsp. pepper
- ✓ 1/2 tsp. garlic powder
- ✓ 4 tbsp. cooking oil
- ✓ 1 tbsp. soy sauce

Cut the bell pepper into approximately 1-inch square pieces. Cut ham into approximately 2-inch square pieces. Heat the oil in a pot, skillet, or wok at the highest stove setting. As the oil is just beginning to smoke, toss in the crushed red pepper. When these have just started to blacken, toss in the bell pepper and ham. Turn constantly, sprinkling in salt, pepper, garlic powder, and soy sauce. Add a little water. Turn frequently for about 2 minutes. Drain and pour into serving bowl. Mix in chili garlic sauce. Serves approximately 4 people.

Stir-Fried Sesame Spinach

Ingredients

- ✓ Fresh bunch of spinach
- ✓ 1/2 tsp. salt
- ✓ 1/8 tsp. black pepper
- ✓ 1/2 tsp. garlic powder
- ✓ 1/2 tsp. soy sauce
- ✓ 1 tsp. sesame oil
- ✓ 2 tbsp. cooking oil

Rinse spinach and cut up into bite-sized pieces. Heat oil in pot, skillet, or wok on the highest stove setting. Spinach cooks in less than 30 seconds after the heat has just begun to smoke, so you may actually turn the stove off after the oil has been heated to this intensity. At this point, toss in spinach, stirring rapidly. As you add the remaining ingredients, continue to stir constantly. Sprinkle in salt, pepper, garlic powder, and soy sauce. After about 30 seconds, when the spinach is just turning from its lighter, raw state to a darker, cooked appearance, pour into a serving bowl. Pour off excess liquid and sprinkle in sesame oil. Serves approximately 4 people.

 # Chinese Noodles

Ingredients

- ✓ 1/2 pound spaghetti noodles
- ✓ 1/4 tsp. salt
- ✓ 1/8 tsp. pepper
- ✓ 2 tbsp. soy sauce
- ✓ 1/4 tsp. garlic powder

Boil enough spaghetti noodles for 4 people. Drain all but a tiny amount of water. Return the pot with the noodles to the stove, keeping heat at the highest setting. Sprinkle in salt, pepper, and garlic powder, stirring constantly. Sprinkle in soy sauce. Stir rapidly for just a few turns. Cover pot for about ten seconds. Uncover pot and stir rapidly for a few turns. Pour into serving bowl. Serves approximately 4 people.

Note: This dish may serve either as the main grain for a dinner, substituting for rice, or it may be turned into a delicious one-bowl meal by adding items such as ham, bell pepper, and onions, at the same time that the spices are added.

 # Spicy Bok Choy Cabbage

Ingredients

- ✓ Bunch of bok choy cabbage
- ✓ 1/4 tsp. salt
- ✓ 1/8 tsp. pepper
- ✓ 1/2 tsp. garlic powder

- ✓ 4 tbsp. cooking oil
- ✓ 1 tbsp. soy sauce
- ✓ 1/2 tsp. chili garlic sauce

Cut cabbage into bite-sized pieces. Heat oil in a pot, skillet, or wok to high. Toss in cabbage pieces, stirring constantly. As you add the remaining ingredients, continue to stir constantly. Sprinkle in salt and pepper, followed by the garlic powder. Pour in soy sauce, turning constantly. Continue to stir rapidly for about 90 seconds or until the cabbage is tender but still firm. Drain liquid and remove to serving bowl. Stir in the 1/2 teaspoon (a full teaspoon if you dare!) of chili garlic powder. Serves approximately 4 people.

Garlic Shrimp with Onions and Bell Pepper

Ingredients

- ✓ 12-oz. package of large, precooked, peeled shrimp
- ✓ 1/8 medium-sized onion, diced
- ✓ 1 green, red, or yellow bell pepper
- ✓ 1/4 tsp. salt
- ✓ 1/8 tsp. pepper
- ✓ 1/2 tsp. garlic powder
- ✓ 4 tbsp. cooking oil
- ✓ 1 tbsp. soy sauce

Using a sharp knife, cut the tails off of enough large shrimp to serve 4 people. Cut the bell pepper into approximately 1-inch square pieces. Heat cooking oil in pot, skillet, or wok at the highest stove setting. As oil is just beginning to smoke, toss in onion and sprinkle in garlic powder, stirring constantly. As you add the remaining ingredients, continue to stir constantly. Immediately toss in the shrimp and bell pepper pieces. Sprinkle in salt and pepper, followed by the soy sauce. Add a small amount of water and cover for about 15 seconds. Uncover, drain, and remove to serving bowl. Serves approximately 4 people.

Stir-Fried Green Beans

Ingredients

- ✓ 1 10-oz. package of frozen green beans
- ✓ 1/4 tsp. salt
- ✓ 1/8 tsp. garlic powder
- ✓ 4 tbsp. cooking oil
- ✓ 1 tbsp. soy sauce

Heat oil in a pot, skillet, or wok at the highest stove setting. Toss in enough green beans for 4 people, stirring rapidly. As you add the remaining ingredients, continue to stir constantly. Sprinkle in salt, pepper, and garlic powder, then sprinkle in the soy sauce. Add a little water and cover for about 1 minute. Remove from heat, drain, and place in a serving bowl.

Note: This is an adaptation of a dish known in Taiwan as "Four Season Beans." It may also, of course, be made with fresh green beans, but this dish is pleasing using high-quality frozen green beans and fixed in this manner is an exceptionally simple, fast, and tasty dish.

 # Black Pepper Shrimp with Onions

Ingredients

- ✓ 1 package of large, precooked, peeled, frozen shrimp
- ✓ 1/2 medium-sized onion, chopped
- ✓ 4 tbsp. cooking oil
- ✓ 1 tbsp. soy sauce
- ✓ 1/4 tsp. salt
- ✓ 1/8 tsp. pepper
- ✓ 1/4 tsp. garlic powder

Using a sharp knife, cut the tails off the shrimp. Dice about an eighth of a medium-sized onion. Heat cooking oil in a pot, skillet, or wok at the highest setting. Toss in onions with garlic powder, stirring constantly. Toss in shrimp with salt and soy sauce, stirring constantly, followed by the pepper. Remove from heat and place in a serving bowl. Serves approximately 4 people.

Drunken Chicken

Ingredients

- ✓ 1 very large, boneless frozen chicken breast
- ✓ 1/2 cup white cooking wine
- ✓ 1/2 tsp. ginger powder
- ✓ 1/4 tsp. salt

Thaw chicken just enough so it can be cut into thin slices. Place in a medium-sized, microwavable container. Sprinkle in ginger powder and salt. Cover and shake container. Cook in microwave for about 3 minutes, more if necessary to cook thoroughly (but do not overcook). Put chicken in the freezer for about 20 minutes, or long enough to achieve chilled effect without freezing the chicken. Arrange attractively on a serving dish. Serves approximately 4 people.

Note: This is an adaptation of a dish served in Szechwan restaurants in Taiwan. It utilizes the conveniences of a contemporary kitchen while achieving a flavor very similar to the original. The term "drunken" comes from the use of cooking wine, but as with all such dishes, any alcohol disappears as a result of the cooking process.

Spicy Sweet and Sour Cucumbers

Ingredients

- ✓ 1 large cucumber
- ✓ 1/4 tsp. salt
- ✓ 1/8 tsp. pepper
- ✓ 1 tbsp. sugar
- ✓ 4 cups cooking oil
- ✓ 1 tbsp. soy sauce
- ✓ 1 tbsp. apple cider vinegar
- ✓ 1/4 tsp. garlic powder

Cut cucumbers into narrow strips about 2 inches in length. Heat oil in pot, skillet, or wok on the highest setting. As the oil is just beginning to smoke, toss in the cucumber, stirring constantly. As you add the remaining ingredients, continue to stir constantly. Sprinkle in salt, pepper, and garlic powder, followed by the soy sauce and then the vinegar. Sprinkle in sugar. Add a little water and cover for about 15 seconds. When the interior part of the cucumber softens and the green peel remains firm, remove from heat and place in a serving bowl. Serves approximately 4 people.

 # Stir-Fried Cabbage with Shrimp Bits

Ingredients

- ✓ 12 large, frozen, peeled, precooked shrimp
- ✓ 1/3 head of cabbage
- ✓ 1/4 tsp. salt
- ✓ 1/8 tsp. pepper
- ✓ 4 tbsp. cooking oil
- ✓ 1 tbsp. soy sauce

Cut the cabbage into bite-sized pieces. With a sharp knife, cut frozen shrimp pieces into about seven small pieces. Heat oil in a pot, skillet, or wok at the highest setting. As oil is just beginning to smoke, toss in shrimp pieces, stirring rapidly. As you add the remaining ingredients, continue to stir constantly. Sprinkle in soy sauce, stirring rapidly. Add enough water to cover the shrimp. Cover about 15 seconds, and then stir rapidly once more. Add the cabbage pieces, stirring constantly. Sprinkle in salt, pepper, and garlic powder, continuing to stir. Cover for about 90 seconds, or long enough for the cabbage to become tender but still fairly crisp. Stir vigorously, remove from heat, and place in a serving bowl. Serves approximately 4 people.

 # Stir-Fried Rice with Peas and Carrots

Ingredients

- ✓ 1 medium-sized carrot
- ✓ 1/2 cup of frozen peas
- ✓ 1 cup of dry white rice
- ✓ 1/8 medium-sized onion, chopped

- ✓ 2 cups water
- ✓ 1/4 tsp. salt
- ✓ 1/8 tsp. pepper
- ✓ 1/4 tsp. garlic powder
- ✓ 2 tsp. cooking oil
- ✓ 1 tbsp. soy sauce

Dice about an eighth of a medium-sized onion. Cut carrot into small bits. Heat 1 teaspoon of cooking oil in a small pan. Put 1 cup of dry rice along with the onions into pan, stirring rapidly. When the rice appears to be getting slightly crisp (but without blackening or burning either the rice or onions), pour in water. Bring to boil, then reduce heat to low, cover, and cook about 20 minutes. Heat 1 teaspoon oil in separate pot, skillet, or wok. Toss rice into pot with carrots and frozen peas, stirring rapidly for about 30 seconds. Remove from heat and place in a serving bowl. Serves about 4 people.

 # Pork Slices with Fresh Garlic and Onions

Ingredients

- ✓ 3 pork loin steaks, 6 oz. each
- ✓ 1 medium-sized onion
- ✓ 4 cups cooking oil
- ✓ 1/4 tsp. salt
- ✓ 1/8 tsp. pepper
- ✓ 1/2 tsp. garlic powder
- ✓ 1 tbsp. soy sauce
- ✓ 8 medium-sized pieces of fresh garlic clove

Place pork loin steaks in an oven pan and sprinkle with salt, pepper, garlic powder, and soy sauce. Broil the steaks in the oven until done. Remove from the oven and place on a cutting board. Slice the meat into medium-narrow strips about 2 inches long and 1 inch wide. Heat oil in pot, skillet, or wok on highest setting. As oil is just beginning to smoke, toss in fresh garlic and the soy sauce, stirring vigorously. Add a little water and cover for about a minute or until garlic softens. Toss in the onion and sprinkle with salt, pepper, and garlic powder. Toss in pork slices and stir vigorously for about 15 seconds.

Remove from heat and place the pork, onion, and garlic on separate sections of the same serving dish. Serves approximately 4 people.

Note: This recipe is an adaptation of a dish that is very popular among farm families in Taiwan, who actually eat this dish with raw garlic pieces. Most Americans find raw garlic eaten in such large pieces to be too strong, thus the adaptation to a briefly cooked form. The dish as prepared according to the above description is tasty and fundamentally faithful to the rural Taiwanese idea.

 # Pinto Beans in Soy Sauce

Ingredients

- ✓ 2 cups dry pinto beans
- ✓ 4 tsp. soy sauce

Boil pinto beans for about 90 minutes. When the beans are cooked but still rather firm, drain water. Return the pan to the stove, set on high. Pour in soy sauce, stirring rapidly. Cover for about 30 seconds, then uncover, stir rapidly, and remove to serving dish. Serves approximately 4 people.

Note: This is an adaptation of an appetizer or side dish served in city restaurants in Taiwan. It is a simple, tasty compliment to a meal. Another tasty, even simpler side dish is achieved by simply putting a small plate of shelled and salted peanuts on the table.

 # Coriander Chicken

Ingredients

- ✓ 2 large, boneless chicken breasts
- ✓ 1/4 tsp. salt
- ✓ 1/8 tsp. pepper
- ✓ 1/4 tsp. garlic powder
- ✓ 1 bunch fresh coriander (cilantro)
- ✓ 1/8 medium-sized onion, chopped
- ✓ 4 tbsp. cooking oil
- ✓ 1 tbsp. soy sauce

Dice about an eighth of an onion. Thaw chicken breasts just enough to allow cutting. Cut chicken into approximately 1-inch cubes. Cut enough fresh coriander so that you will be able to cover the chicken with it generously when tossed together in a pot, skillet, or wok. Heat oil in the pot at the highest setting. As the oil is just beginning to smoke, toss in chicken, turning rapidly. As you add the remaining ingredients, continue to stir constantly, sprinkling in the salt, pepper, garlic powder, and soy sauce. Toss in the coriander, stirring rapidly. Cover 10 seconds, stir rapidly, remove from heat and place in a serving dish. Serves approximately 4 people.

 # Basil Tomatoes and Onions

Ingredients

- ✓ 1 large fresh tomato
- ✓ 1 whole onion
- ✓ 1 tbsp. fresh chopped or dried basil
- ✓ 1/4 tsp. salt
- ✓ 1/8 tsp. pepper
- ✓ 1/4 tsp. garlic powder
- ✓ 4 tbsp. cooking oil
- ✓ 1 tbsp. soy sauce

Cut 1 whole tomato into approximately 12 medium-thick slices. Cut the onion into several good-sized pieces. Heat oil in pot, skillet, or wok on highest setting. As the oil is just beginning to smoke, toss in the onion and stir rapidly. Continuing to stir constantly as you add the remaining ingredients, first sprinkle in salt and pepper, followed by the garlic powder. Sprinkle in soy sauce. Toss in tomatoes. Cover for 10 seconds, drain most of the liquid, return to stove on highest setting and sprinkle in fresh or dried basil. Turn briskly for about 30 seconds, remove from heat, and place in a serving bowl. Serves approximately 4 people.

Spicy Sweet and Sour Cabbage

Ingredients

- ✓ 1/3 of a head of cabbage
- ✓ 1 tsp. apple cider vinegar
- ✓ 1/4 tsp. salt
- ✓ 1/8 tsp. pepper
- ✓ 1/2 tsp. garlic powder
- ✓ 1 tsp. sugar
- ✓ 10 crushed red pepper pieces
- ✓ 4 tbsp. cooking oil
- ✓ 2 tbsp. soy sauce

Cut the cabbage into bite-sized pieces. Heat the crushed red pepper in pot, skillet, or wok on the highest setting. When the red pepper has just started to blacken, toss in cabbage pieces, turning briskly. Continuing stirring rapidly as you add the remaining ingredients. Sprinkle in salt and pepper, garlic powder and soy sauce. Pour in the apple cider vinegar and then sprinkle in sugar. Add a little water and cover for about 45 seconds. Uncover and stir rapidly once again. Cabbage should be tender but crisp. Remove from heat and place in a serving bowl. Serves approximately 4 people.

Chicken and Mushrooms

Ingredients

- ✓ 1 large, frozen chicken breast
- ✓ 1/8 medium-sized onion, chopped
- ✓ 8-oz can of whole mushrooms
- ✓ 1/4 tsp. salt
- ✓ 1/8 tsp. pepper
- ✓ 1/4 tsp. garlic powder
- ✓ 1 tbsp. soy sauce
- ✓ 4 tbsp. cooking oil

Thaw chicken just enough to allow cutting. Cut chicken into approximately 1-inch cubes. Separate stem from each mushroom but otherwise keep mushrooms whole and save the stems. Heat cooking oil in a pot, skillet, or wok at the highest setting. As oil is just beginning to smoke, toss in chicken and onion together, turning rapidly. Continue to stir rapidly as you add the remaining ingredients. Sprinkle in a generous amount of garlic powder, followed by salt and pepper. Toss in mushrooms, including stems, sprinkling more garlic powder over the mushrooms. Sprinkle in soy sauce. Add a little water and cover for about 15 seconds. Remove from heat and place in a serving bowl. Serves approximately 4 people.

Beef and Green Pepper Strips

Ingredients

- ✓ 2-lb beef chuck roast
- ✓ 1 green bell pepper
- ✓ 1/4 tsp. salt
- ✓ 1/8 tsp. pepper
- ✓ 1/4 tsp. garlic powder
- ✓ 4 tbsp. cooking oil
- ✓ 1 tbsp. soy sauce

Place chuck roast on a greased roasting pan and sprinkle with salt, pepper, and garlic powder. Roast in 350-degree oven until done. While the beef is roasting, cut green pepper into pencil-thin strips. When the roast is done, remove and slice, also into pencil-thin strips about 2 inches long. Heat oil in pot, skillet, or wok to high. Toss in beef and green pepper strips, stirring briskly as you add salt, pepper, garlic powder, and soy sauce. Add a little water and cover for 30 seconds. Remove from heat and place in a serving bowl. Serves approximately 4 people.

Homestyle Roast Beef

Ingredients

- ✓ 2-lb. beef chuck roast
- ✓ 1/2 medium-sized onion
- ✓ 1 stalk celery
- ✓ 1 medium-sized carrot
- ✓ 1/4 tsp. salt
- ✓ 1/8 tsp. pepper
- ✓ 1/4 tsp. garlic powder
- ✓ 1 tbsp. soy sauce
- ✓ 4 tbsp. cooking oil

Place chuck roast on a greased roasting pan and sprinkle with salt, pepper, and garlic powder. Roast in a 350-degree oven until done. While the beef is roasting, cut carrots, celery, and onions into pencil-thin strips. When the roast is done, remove and slice, also into pencil-thin strips. Heat oil in pot, skillet, or wok on highest setting. As oil is just beginning to smoke, toss in beef, carrot, celery, and onion strips, stirring briskly as you add salt and pepper. Add garlic powder and soy sauce, stirring briskly. Add a little water and cover for 30 seconds. Remove from heat and place in a serving dish. Serves approximately 4 people.

Mongolian Barbecue

Ingredients

- ✓ 8-oz sirloin steak
- ✓ 1 green bell pepper
- ✓ 1 carrot
- ✓ 1/5 head of cabbage
- ✓ 1 onion
- ✓ 1 tomato
- ✓ Half a medium-sized cucumber
- ✓ 10 crushed red pepper pieces

- ✓ 1/4 tsp. ground ginger
- ✓ 1/4 tsp. salt
- ✓ 1/8 tsp. pepper
- ✓ 1/4 tsp. garlic powder
- ✓ 1 tsp. sugar
- ✓ 1 tbsp. apple cider vinegar
- ✓ 1 tbsp. soy sauce
- ✓ 4 tbsp. cooking oil

Place steak in an oven pan and sprinkle with generous amount of soy sauce. Turn the steak around in the pan and return to original side. Sprinkle in salt, pepper, and garlic powder. Broil until meat is rare. Meanwhile, cut green pepper, carrot, cabbage, onion, cucumber, and tomato into bite-sized pieces. When meat is done, place on a cutting board and cut into thin strips about 2 inches long and 1 inch wide. Heat a few crushed red pepper pieces in pot, skillet, or wok at the highest setting. When red pepper is just turning black, toss in onions, stirring briskly for about 15 seconds. Continue to stir rapidly as you add the remaining ingredients, first tossing in the green pepper, carrot, cabbage, and cucumber pieces. Then sprinkle in salt, pepper, and ginger. Sprinkle in garlic power. Pour in apple cider vinegar and sugar. Toss in steak pieces, and turn briskly with other items. Just as the meat turns from red to brown, toss in tomato pieces for a brief stir before removing to serving bowl. Spoon into individual serving bowls. Serves approximately 4 people.

Note: This dish is an adaptation of "Mongolian Barbecue," which despite its name, seems to have gained its contemporary form and popularity in the city restaurants of Taiwan. You can now find Mongolian Barbecue in many cities of the United States. In these, as in Taiwan, you choose the items that you want in your dish. Steak is only one of the meat possibilities. Often you can choose lamb, probably truer to any version of this that the Mongols historically would have eaten. After you have chosen the uncooked items that you want from a buffet, the cooks stir the ingredients on a grill shaped like a huge drum. Try one of these restaurants if your family agrees. You'll find that the taste is similar to that you'll get by following the version of this recipe.

Sweet and Sour Chicken

Ingredients

- ✓ 2 frozen chicken breasts
- ✓ 1/4 cup honey
- ✓ 1/4 cup apple cider vinegar
- ✓ 1 tbsp. sweet basil
- ✓ 3 cups flour
- ✓ 3 cups cooking oil
- ✓ 1 tbsp. ground ginger
- ✓ 1 tbsp. salt
- ✓ 1/2 tbsp. pepper
- ✓ 1 tbsp. garlic powder
- ✓ 1 fresh pineapple
- ✓ Bowl of milk

Prepare a mixture of flour, sweet basil, ground ginger, garlic powder, salt, and pepper. Have a bowl of milk ready for dipping. Cut partially frozen chicken breasts into bite-sized pieces. Heat oil in a skillet to cover chicken pieces once you have tossed them into the skillet. Set the temperature at medium-hot (about halfway between medium and the hottest temperature). Dip the chicken pieces one by one into the milk, then into the flour and seasoning mixture. It is fine if the meat is still partially frozen; pieces this small will thaw rapidly while frying and the formation of a crust at this temperature will indicate that the chicken is done.

Place the pieces in the skillet. When the flour turns golden and all of the dry flour on the exposed side turns moist, turn the chicken over. After a couple of minutes, you can begin to move the chicken around in the skillet, striving for a uniform crustiness. Don't overcook. Small pieces like these will cook quickly. After both sides of a chicken breast have formed a crust, remove it from the skillet with a slit spoon or spatula. If done correctly, most pieces should be ready at about the same time. Have a double thickness of two-ply paper towels ready and place the chicken pieces down on them to drain.

Cut the fresh pineapple into chunks that can be easily picked up with chopsticks. Heat honey and some apple cider vinegar in a pot, skillet, or wok. Slide chicken and pineapple in rapid succession into the pot or wok, give several quick turns, remove from heat, and serve.

Stir-Fried Carrots and Broccoli

Ingredients

- ✓ 2 medium to large carrots
- ✓ 1 bunch of broccoli
- ✓ 1 tbsp. soy sauce
- ✓ 1/4 tsp. salt
- ✓ 1/8 tsp. pepper
- ✓ 4 tbsp. cooking oil

Slice carrots into strips about 1-1/2 inches long. Cut broccoli so that there are a combination of pieces, dominated by the flower, but also adding some of the stem. Heat oil in a pot, skillet, or wok at the highest setting. Toss in carrots and sprinkle garlic powder, salt and pepper over them. Stir. Add soy sauce. Stir. Add a bit of water. Stir frequently. When you see that the carrots have just begun to soften, toss in the broccoli. Stir. Add a touch more garlic powder, salt, pepper, directed toward the broccoli. Stir. Add a bit of soy sauce, again aiming for the broccoli. After the broccoli has had just enough time to absorb the spices and gain some tenderness but retain its crunchiness, remove from heat and place on a serving plate. Serves approximately four people.

Spicy Sesame Beef

Ingredients

- ✓ 2-lb beef chuck roast
- ✓ 1 tbsp. soy sauce
- ✓ 1/4 tsp. salt
- ✓ 1/8 tsp. pepper
- ✓ 1/4 tsp. garlic powder
- ✓ 2 tsp. sesame oil
- ✓ 2 tsp. pretoasted sesame seeds
- ✓ 4 tbsp. cooking oil

Cook the chuck roast in the oven. Place on center rack in a roaster or heavy pan. Sprinkle with soy sauce, then sprinkle with salt, pepper, and garlic powder, covering all sides. Bake or roast at 350 degrees for about 1 hour or until medium rare. Remove from the oven and place on a cutting board. Let the meat cool for about 10 minutes. Slice beef into thin strips, about 1-1/2 inches long.

Heat oil in a pot, skillet, or wok at highest setting. Toss in beef strips, sprinkle with soy sauce, stir. In rapid succession, sprinkle in salt, pepper, and garlic powder, stirring rapidly. As the meat turns from medium rare to brown, remove to a container with a lid. Sprinkle in sesame seeds to uniformly cover the meat, then do the same with the sesame oil. Put a lid on the container, shake vigorously, and place on a serving plate. Serves approximately four people.

 # Stir-Fried Snow Peas

Ingredients

- ✓ 2 cups snow peas
- ✓ 1/4 tsp. salt
- ✓ 1/8 tsp. pepper
- ✓ 1/4 tsp. garlic powder
- ✓ 1 tbsp. soy sauce
- ✓ 4 tbsp. cooking oil
- ✓ 1/4 c. water

Cut snow pea pods to remove the stringy part that runs down the side and cut the tips off the pods at both ends. Heat enough oil to cover the bottom of a pot, skillet, or wok with a thin layer. Toss in snow peas, stirring rapidly. Continue to stir rapidly as you sprinkle in soy sauce, about a quarter cup of water, then the salt, pepper, and garlic powder in rapid succession. Cover for about 15 seconds, stir rapidly, and remove to serving dish. This is an extremely fast dish to prepare, especially once the snow peas have been prepared. The snow peas should be cooked long enough to absorb the spices but should still be firm when removed from heat.

Spicy Chicken with Peanuts

Ingredients

- ✓ 2 frozen chicken breasts
- ✓ 1/4 medium-sized onion, diced
- ✓ 1 tbsp. apple cider vinegar
- ✓ 1/4 c. cooking wine
- ✓ 1 tsp. crushed Szechwan peppercorns
- ✓ 1/4 tsp. salt
- ✓ 1/8 tsp. pepper
- ✓ 1/4 tsp. garlic powder
- ✓ 1/2 tsp. ground ginger
- ✓ 10 crushed red pepper pieces
- ✓ 1 tbsp. soy sauce
- ✓ 3 cups cooking oil
- ✓ 2 tbsp. corn starch

Slice partially thawed chicken into bite-sized pieces. Mix corn starch with enough water to make a thick liquid batter. Place chicken in bowl and pour the corn starch batter over it. Mix in peppercorns and stir thoroughly. Heat oil in a pot, skillet, or wok at a medium-high setting as you would to fry chicken. Toss chicken in to fry, cooking until the batter on the chicken starts to turn a golden brown. Remove to paper towel to absorb excess oil.

Remove excess oil from the pan, leaving only a small amount, just enough to cover the bottom of the pan. Heat crushed red peppers until they are just beginning to turn black. Toss in ground ginger and diced onions, turning rapidly. Continue to turn rapidly as you add enough soy sauce to cover the chicken lightly, then add apple cider vinegar and cooking wine, stirring constantly. Sprinkle in salt, pepper, and garlic powder. Sprinkle in enough peanuts to mix well with chicken, stir rapidly, remove from heat, and place in a serving dish.

Stir-Fried Mixed Vegetables

Ingredients

- ✓ 1 yellow squash
- ✓ 1 zucchini squash
- ✓ 1 small onion
- ✓ 1 tomato
- ✓ 1/4 tsp. salt
- ✓ 1/8 tsp. pepper
- ✓ 1/4 tsp. garlic powder
- ✓ 1/4 tsp. sugar
- ✓ 1 tbsp. soy sauce
- ✓ 4 tbsp. cooking oil

Slice the yellow squash into thin strips, about 1 1/2 inches long and ¾ inch wide. Do the same for the zucchini squash. Repeat this slicing process for the onion and for the tomato. Heat cooking oil on highest stove setting. As oil is just beginning to smoke, toss in onions and stir rapidly while adding soy sauce, a small amount of water, salt, pepper, and garlic powder. Toss in both yellow and zucchini squash, stirring rapidly and adding soy sauce, salt, pepper, and garlic powder. Toss in tomato and cook for just 15 seconds, adding sugar to the whole mixture while stirring rapidly. Remove from heat and place in a serving dish.

Honey-Fried Chicken Drummies

Ingredients

- ✓ 1 package of frozen chicken wing drummies (about 1 1/4 pounds)
- ✓ 1/4 cup honey
- ✓ 1/4 cup apple cider vinegar
- ✓ 3 cups flour
- ✓ Bowl of milk
- ✓ 1 tbsp. sweet basil
- ✓ 1 tbsp. salt
- ✓ 1/4 tbsp. pepper

- ✓ 1 tbsp. ground ginger
- ✓ 1 tbsp. soy sauce
- ✓ 3 cups cooking oil

Prepare flour mixture with salt, pepper, garlic powder, sweet basil, and ginger. Dip each drummie in milk, then toss the drummies into the bowl with the flour mixture, covering each individually. Heat cooking oil in a pot, skillet, or wok on a medium-high stove setting to prepare to fry the chicken. Place chicken pieces into the hot oil and cook until a golden brown crust forms. Remove to a paper towel for draining. Remove the oil from pot, skillet, or wok, then wash and dry the utensil thoroughly. Heat honey and a small amount of apple cider vinegar in the pan. Toss in drummies, stirring rapidly until thoroughly covered with the honey and apple cider vinegar mixture. Remove from heat and place in a serving bowl.

 # Taiwanese Scrambled Egg

Ingredients

- ✓ 1 egg
- ✓ 1/8 medium-sized onion, diced
- ✓ 1/4 tsp. salt
- ✓ 1/8 tsp. pepper
- ✓ 1/2 tbsp. soy sauce
- ✓ 3 tbsp. cooking oil

Beat egg, sprinkle in salt and pepper, and then beat again briskly. Mix the diced onion into the egg mixture, again beating briskly. Heat cooking oil in a pot, skillet, or wok at a medium stove setting. Pour the egg into the oil and cook flat, like a pancake. Sprinkle in about half of the soy sauce. As the egg starts to become firm, flip it over and sprinkle with the rest of the soy sauce. As the egg firms on the other side, remove and place in a serving dish. Serves 1.

Index

Phoenix Mountain, 104
Popular Tales from Taiwan (*Taiwan minjian gushi*), x
presidential election in Taiwan, 5
    of 1996, 5
    of 2000, 5
Puyuma (aborigine group), 1
    language, 1

Qianlong, Emperor, 124–125
Qing dynasty (1644–1912), 3, 4, 37, 115–17, 124, 132
Quanzhou, xi, 3–6, 25–26, 127
    people of, xi, 3–6
    district (of Fujian province), 25–26, 127

Red-Haired Well, 121
Republic of China (official name for the government or nation of Taiwan), 7
Republic of Taiwan (name favored by some on Taiwan), 7
river spirit, 57–59

Saisiat (aborigine group), 1
    aborigine language of, 1
Sea Dragon King, 97
shao tian (to burn up heaven; also, to overcome difficulty), 92
Shilin District (of Taibei), 10
Son of Heaven (one of the references to the emperor of China), 92
Spaniards, ix, 3
stone (commemorative) pillars, 124
Stone Well's Foot, 79
Sun Moon Lake (Big Lake Shuishe), 131–32. *See also* Big Lake Shuishe
    tree god of, 131

Tablet of the Divine Master, 51. *See also* Tablet of the Divine Mother; Taiwan ancestral tablet
Tablet of the Honorable Mother, 51. *See also* Tablet of the Divine Master; Taiwan ancestral tablet
Taibei, 6–7, 107, 127
Tainan City, 7, 65, 68, 124–25
Tainan County, x, 79
Taiyang Pian, 43–47
Taiwan Strait, 4
Taiwanese ancestral tablet, 49. *See also* Tablet of the Divine Master; Tablet of the Honorable Mother
Taiwanese language, 1, 6
Taizhong (Taichung), 7
Taroko (aborigine group), 1
    aborigine language of, 1
Taya, (aborigine group), 1
    aborigine language of, 1
Ten Thousand-Mile Ox, 98
Thao (aborigine group), 1
    aboriginal language of, 1
Thousand-Mile Stallion, 98
Tian Lo, 92
Tiger-Nosed Lion, 89
Tree God (of Sun Moon Lake), 131
Tsou (aborigine group), 1, 132
    aboriginal language of, 1

United States, influence on Taiwan, 7
    bombing of Japanese-held Taiwan during World War II, 128

Wanhua District (of Taibei), 127–28
White Horse Mateng, 79–80
White Rice Pot, 29
World War II (1939–1945), impact on Taiwan, 5, 128
Wu Changzuo, 132

Xu Wanqi, Dr., 118–19

Yami (aborigine group), 1, 5
    aboriginal language of, 1
Yu Zaixiang, 38
Yu Zhi, 15–18

Zhang Chayuan, 128
Zhang Dacai, 91
Zhang Fushan, 15–16

Zhangzhou, xi, 3–6
    people of, xi, 3–6
Zheng Chenggong, xi, 4, 103–104, 122.
       See also Guoxingye; Koxinga
Zhenjie fang (Arches of
       Never-Failing Integrity), 37.
       See also Arches of
       Never-Failing Integrity
Zhenluan Temple, 37
Zhiwuye, 43, 46–47
zhongzi (rice tamales), 26

About the Author

Gary Marvin Davison has been an educator, historian, and teller of tales for thirty years. He began his career at Pinkston High School in inner-city Dallas during 1973–1975 and since that time has taught at a variety of locations. He has worked to help prisoners get their high school equivalency certificates; taught English as a Second Language in Taiwan; served as a college-level instructor teaching courses on China, Japan, and East Asia; and for well over a decade now, he has been a teacher and tutoring program coordinator of at-risk and inner city young people in Minneapolis.

Davison holds a Ph.D. in Chinese history (University of Minnesota, 1993) and is the author of three previous books. He collaborated with six other authors to write a world history textbook, *A World History: Links across Time and Place* (McDougal-Littell, 1988) and with co-author Barbara Reed to write *Culture and Customs of Taiwan* (Greenwood, 1998). His most recent book prior to this volume was *A Short History of Taiwan: The Case for Independence* (Praeger, 2003). He is currently working on three projects that symbolize his eclectic interests: one is an update of his dissertation on the contemporary economic history of Taiwan's farmers; the other two projects flow from his interest in African American history.

Davison is a frequent presence as a volunteer in the public schools, where he both assists students with academic assignments and tells stories of his own creation, as well as tales told by others. His deep interest in the power of well-told tales to convey important information about people in a variety of cultures gave rise to this volume.

Recent Titles in the World Folklore Series

Additional titles in this series can be found at www.lu.com